D1096280

FAMOUS MODERN ARTISTS

FAMOUS MO

A Chanticleer Press Edition

DERN ARTISTS

FROM CÉZANNE TO POP ART

Charlotte Willard

With 95 reproductions, including 50 in color

PLATT & MUNK, Publishers
New York

HM 53

I wish to thank David Ignatow for his supporting comments, Connie Sullivan for her invaluable editing and picture research, Duney Katzman for editorial research and Abigail Little for a precise and patient job of typing.

Published in 1971 by PLATT & MUNK, a division of Questor Education Products Company.

Planned and produced by Chanticleer Press, New York.

Library of Congress Catalog Number: 72-151241.

Printed by Amilcare Pizzi, S.p.A., Milano, Italy.

CONTENTS

PREFACE

In *Alice in Wonderland*, Lewis Carroll points out that there is a difference between the name of a thing and what the thing really is. Art historians, critics and sometimes artists themselves have given us many names of kinds of art—such as Post-Impressionism, Fauvism, Surrealism and Expressionism—that do not reveal much about the paintings themselves and may even confuse us.

In this book I have tried to tell what the art really is by translating these labels into simple, more meaningful language. Fauvism, for example, has been translated into "The Triumph of Color," Expressionism to "Painters Who Freed Their Emotions," Surrealism to "Dreams and Nightmares," and Op Art to "Paintings Move." I have also dealt with some of the psychological roots of modern art, its emotional basis, its relationship to science and inventions.

Other themes explore the modern artist's relationship to his work and to the times in which he lived. In "Inventors and Discoverers," Cézanne, Picasso and Pollock show us new ways of looking at the world around us. Ben Shahn and Andrew Wyeth give us what I call a "Portrait of Modern Man," and Léger and Lichtenstein try to reconcile "Art and the Machine." These artists often met with violent protest from a public that was not prepared to accept their revolutionary ideas and visions.

Above all, my purpose has been to eliminate obstacles between the reader and his involvement with the paintings themselves. I have tried to strip art of some of the mystifying language surrounding it with the hope that this will lead to a greater understanding and deeper enjoyment of modern painting.

INVENTORS AND DISCOVERERS

All too often an artist is pictured as an unruly genius who waits for an inspiration to send him into a frenzy of paint splashing. We rarely think of artists as great inventors or discoverers. Yet if we look up the word "invention" in a dictionary, we find that it is "something thought up, something originated by experiment; a discovery." The great painters have always done just that. Great artists, like great scientists, are rarely satisfied with things as they are, or with what others have discovered. They are always seeking to find ways to improve methods of painting, to describe the real world.

This inventive urge is not new. Before the Van Eycks (artists who lived in the fifteenth century), painters used to mix pigments with water or egg white. Once this paint was put on canvas it could not be changed. The Van Eycks tried mixing pigments* with oil and thereby changed the history of painting. Oil paints were more lasting than water colors. Most important, oil paints allowed an artist to paint over his mistakes or even to rub out a painting and begin again.

Paolo Uccello, a painter of the early Renaissance,* and a good mathematician, applied the rules of geometry to painting and invented perspective.* Following his rules, paintings acquired depth; and objects and figures in the distance appear much as we see them in real life. It was not by accident that Uccello revised our view of space in a picture decades before Columbus revised our view of space in the world.

In our own time our attention is again focused on space—the outer space of the astronauts and the vast inner spaces of man. Modern artists like Cézanne, Picasso, Pollock and Dubuffet have all made many great inventions in this area of art.

* Term defined in Glossary

PAUL CÉZANNE

At eighteen, Paul Cézanne already knew that he wanted to be a painter, but his father, a banker, wouldn't hear of it. Paul dutifully prepared for law school, but after a three-year battle with his father he finally set out for Paris to study art. Dark, heavy set, with a full black beard, Cézanne looked more like a laborer than an artist. Already a stubborn, silent young man, he had a hard time getting along with people. Yet he could be a loyal and warm friend, and he revered the artist Pissarro, with whom he studied.

Cézanne kept sending his paintings to the French Academy for their annual Salon* exhibit, but the Academy judges regularly turned them down. He simply kept on working. It was not until 1874, when he was already thirty-five years old, that his work was shown in a group exhibition. It was singled out for violent criticism. A typical comment was: "Monsieur Cézanne can only be a kind of madman afflicted with a delirium while painting." Père Tanguy, who sold artists' supplies, gave Cézanne paints in exchange for his paintings and showed a few of his paintings in his shop. After

Tanguy's death the paintings were auctioned off for a few dollars.

All this time Cézanne had lived like a hermit, permitting himself only the barest necessities, but on the death of his father in 1886 he inherited a large fortune. He spent the rest of his life painting in peace. Only in 1906, two weeks before he died, were his paintings included in the Salon d'Independents* exhibition.

A NEW WAY OF SEEING

Cézanne did not want to copy reality. He wanted to invent picture symbols for it—a visual vocabulary. Just as the word "apple" represents the fruit, he wanted to find visual symbols that would stand for people, objects and nature.

We know that sometimes a photograph taken in light that is too weak or too strong distorts our features, and we do not recognize ourselves. The photograph does not catch the essential form of our face. It is this essential form that Cézanne tried to portray. He wanted to put down the basic appearance of an object or a person that makes us recognize a tree as a tree, and a man as a man, no matter what light falls on them. In his search for essential form he decided that the cone, the cylinder and the sphere were the forms behind all objective reality. Another great discovery was the use of contrasting colors—warm colors like red or orange

SELF-PORTRAIT (left)
In this picture Cézanne's sullen expression and his eyes, which seem to look at nothing, clearly tell us of his disappointments, his isolation and his stubbornness.

BOY IN A RED VEST (right)
Cézanne treated the human body as an object. He translated it into geometric shapes so that it might better fit into a composition in which every element was given equal attention and emphasis. He created the illusion of depth by color alone and by reducing everything to the shape of a cone, a cylinder or a sphere, he gave his portraits a monumental solidity.

against cool colors like blue or green, deep shades against light shades, so that he could even make light colors recede and dark colors advance, depending on the colors he used near them. He wanted to create the illusion of depth and solidity by color alone. No wonder it took him months to paint a bowl of apples or a seated figure.

Cézanne went on to other discoveries. He painted as we actually see. He knew that after we have grasped the essential form* of a thing such as a table, we do not bother to look at all the elements of every table. Even these discoveries did not satisfy him. He wanted to paint the changing life of growing or living things—even the nuclear activity in supposedly inanimate objects. In his later paintings the outlines of things are all blurred by overlapping brush strokes; the forms seem to be alive and constantly changing. His paintings surprise us at every turn. We cannot anticipate what we will see next in them, so that we study his canvases as we would a living thing.

Cézanne's early work was highly emotional, almost "Expressionistic" (see Chapter 3). After studying the outside world he was able to bring his own strong emotions under the control of his intelligence. With this union of feeling, intelligence and constant invention, he laid the foundation for many later art movements such as Cubism* and Expressionism* and for much of our thinking about modern art.

THE CARD PLAYERS (above)
Among Cézanne's most famous paintings of
people is the series of canvases he did of a
group of French peasants playing cards. Here
again he builds his figures out of cylinders,
cones and spheres.

STILL LIFE
WITH BASKET OF APPLES (left)
After he defines the essential form of the
table, the cloth and the basket of apples,
Cézanne distorts their shapes and breaks
their continuity of form in order to make
our eyes move from one area of the painting
to another. Here he interrupts the edge of
the tabletop with a napkin and continues it
at a different level.

MONTE SAINTE-VICTOIRE
Cézanne's later canvases became
almost abstract. Instead of using
classic perspective and "modeling"
with line and shadow in this mountain
landscape, he used planes of color. He
had discovered that colors not only
become darker the farther they are
from us but actually change in shade.
As it recedes, orange turns to red, and
yellow to green. By slanting the
patches of color in various directions
he achieves three-dimensional solidity
and depth.

PABLO PICASSO

Pablo Picasso was born in Malaga, Spain. His father, an art teacher, gave the boy his only lessons in art. When Pablo, at fifteen, applied for entrance to the Academy of Art in Barcelona, he was given a test that was supposed to take a month—and passed it in one day! Winning a prize in the National Exhibition at Madrid at eighteen seemed easy and natural for the young painter.

For a while Picasso worked for magazines as an illustrator and art editor. He began traveling back and forth to Paris. Soon he settled in Paris and threw himself into the free life of the artists' quarter.

Because he believed that all artists must imitate everyone, his early work looked successively like that of Velásquez, El Greco, Van Gogh and other artists. Critics dismissed him as a mere copier. By 1907 he had absorbed everything he wanted from others and at twenty-five he produced the masterpiece, *The Young Women of Avignon*—the first in a tradition-smashing style that was soon to be named "Cubism." Though he worked incessantly,

night and day, he did not shun life. He had many women companions and models whom he painted. Collectors began to buy his works. He kept pouring out illustrations for books as well as sets and costumes for the Russian ballet. By 1921 he had created his Cubist masterpiece *The Three Musicians*.

When the Spanish Civil War broke out, he vowed never to return to Spain while Franco was dictator. "Paintings are not made to decorate apartments," he said. "They are instruments of war against brutality and darkness." So he painted his *Guernica*, a shattering criticism of the dehumanizing nature of war.

Even before the end of World War II he was recognized as a great painter, master of many styles.* After the war he moved to southern France and added ceramics to his other interests. Today, one of the world's richest men, like an endless fountain of genius he is still making sculptures, ceramics and etchings in all the styles he invented in his lifetime.

CREATING NEW WORLDS

Picasso's whole life as an artist has been, and continues to be, a series of great inventions and discoveries. As a young man living among the poor and miserable in Madrid and Paris, he painted them not as picturesque subjects for art but as human beings who were the saints and martyrs of our society. Because he used only shades of blue—the color of divinity and the color of misery—this is called his "Blue Period." Later, as his life became more secure, he turned the color of his world to "rose." Beautiful huge gods and goddesses of ancient Greece and Rome were given a new life by his feeling for classical art.*

Studying all the cultures of the world and all their arts, he turned to archeology, technology, nature, even mathematics for images and ideas. Early Spanish sculptures, African masks and the work of Cézanne led him to one of his greatest inventions—Cubism. Segments of triangles, the cone and the sphere—

the basic geometry Cézanne felt was behind all appearances—gave Picasso his forms. Carrying forward Cézanne's work, he invented a system of painting that reduced figures and objects to flattened two-dimensional geometric shapes.

Other inventions, such as collage,* were teeming in Picasso's brain. Collages were pictures made by pasting scraps of paper, rags, rope, wire and newspaper on canvas or board, sometimes with a figure drawn or painted over the assembled material. Reality and the artist's representation of it were fused so that the outside world and the inner imagination of the artist could become one pictorial image.

For a time Picasso joined the Surrealists,* who set out to express our dreams and nightmares (see Chapter 4). By breaking up the human body and combining the pieces with furniture, tools or plant life, Surrealists transformed natural objects and figures according to their own wild imaginings.

FAMILY OF ACROBATS (above)
Here Picasso begins to mix the somber shades of his "blue" period with rose and earth colors and has replaced the downtrodden beggars of his earlier paintings with clowns and acrobats.

THE YOUNG WOMEN OF AVIGNON (left)
Inspired by Cézanne and African sculpture, with this painting Picasso launched "Cubism" and made us aware of the geometric forms behind everyday reality. For the first time we are shown the profile and front view of the face at the same time, and the nude figures of the women become a series of flattened planes that have nothing to do with ordinary appearances. The bowl of fruit in the foreground is flattened so much that it seems to be pasted on the surface of the canvas.

Picasso's figures, made up of distorted unnatural forms, were rooted in Cubism. Surrealist ideas to him were just another step forward towards liberating his art from traditional rules. Aiming at a direct path to our emotions, Picasso next invaded the unconscious for symbols that move us. The bull and the horse became his picture language for man and woman, brutality and tenderness, and many other ideas.

More inventions were to come. Shuttling between Cubism, classicism, collage, book illustration and straight representational art,* Picasso painted *Guernica*. Guernica was a Spanish town wiped out in an air-raid by German Nazis and Italian Fascists who opposed the Spanish Republic. Beyond horror or hate, more than any bloody painting of battle, this one makes us experience the inhuman brutality of war.

Like a god who must keep on creating regardless of destruction and chaos, Picasso, after the war, went on working his inventions into more peaceful and joyful forms. He painted lyrical landscapes* of southern France, abstractions, beautiful women, still lifes,* gentle symbols of peace. Like the sun, he makes life from everything he sees and touches.

GIRL BEFORE A MIRROR (above)
Picasso redesigned the human face and figure and invented a new way of looking at the world—showing the front and back, the outside and an x-ray portrait of a figure or object all at the same time. Here he breaks up the body into sweeping curves, circles and bold patterns. Pieces of bright, glossy color vibrate within a heavy black outline.

THREE MUSICIANS (left)
A landmark in the history of art, this picture sums up Picasso's inventions in Cubism. By completely flattening the figures and laying one surface or plane over another, his figures seem to move back and forth so that we are never quite sure which is in front and which is in back. The group of gay street musicians are no longer solid human beings but shifting paper dolls that sing to the endless originality of their creator.

17

GUERNICA

It has been said that no picture portrays the violence of our age so completely as this one. Using all the pictorial language he had invented, Picasso makes us hear and feel, as well as see, with our eyes. We experience the agony of the screaming woman holding her dead child, the terror of the dying horse, the horror of death falling from the sky.

MARCEL DUCHAMP

1887–1968

Marcel Duchamp abandoned painting at the age of thirty-six because, as he said, he had run out of ideas and didn't want to repeat himself. Born in France, he was one of three extraordinarily talented sons. After studying in Paris, young Duchamp became a daring experimenter. When he showed his painting, *Nude Descending a Staircase*, at a major exhibition in Paris it caused such a disturbance that he was asked to remove it. It had an even more explosive effect at the Armory Show in New York in 1913, and became a symbol of the revolution of modern art.

Moving to New York City in 1915, Duchamp restlessly continued to seek new forms of expression. He used a great variety of materials. He sometimes took an object, such as a shovel, signed it and called it "In Advance of a Broken Arm," explaining that he was playing the "role of the artistic clown." Withdrawing from the public eye and devoting much of his time to chess, the wiry, genial Frenchman lived in the United States until his death.

ART OF IDEAS

Because he had older brothers who were established artists when he was still a student, Marcel Duchamp was exposed to such modern modes of painting as Impressionism* and Cubism. When he finally decided to be a painter he rejected all of them and set out to change our ideas about art. Feeling that art had been aimed at the eye, Duchamp proposed that it should be aimed at the mind and should be shocking and original. What he found most shocking in the world around him was the way machines dominate our lives. "I believe that art is the only form of activity," he declared, "by which man as he is manifests himself as a real individual."

His ready-mades, such as a reproduction of Leonardo's *Mona Lisa* decorated with a goatee and a moustache, were other sledgehammer blows at classic notions of art. These ready-mades make him the obvious ancestor of Pop art*, just as his circular paintings rotated by motors are the grandfathers of much Op art* of the 1960's.

NUDE DESCENDING
A STAIRCASE (left)

Duchamp painted this picture, which looks like a slow-motion film of a robot walking down a circular staircase, with great patience and humor. To emphasize its intellectual content he avoided the appeal of color and used neutral tones. Most important of all, he carried Cubism, which sees all forms in terms of planes, a step further by introducing the idea of motion into painting. The picture created a furor. "I am really trying to invent instead of merely trying to express myself," Duchamp explained.

BRIDE STRIPPED BARE BY
HER BACHELORS (far left)

In this painting Duchamp made an important visual and intellectual statement about machines. The bride hangs from the sky and through her antennae communicates with her nine suitors, all dressed in red. A mechanical image of desire and frustration, the picture mocks "modern love." Cold and technical rather than emotional, the only possible bond between the "lovers" is electricity.

21

JACKSON POLLOCK 1912–1956

Born in Cody, Wyoming, Jackson Pollock became interested in art while still in his teens. Leaving high school in Los Angeles before he was graduated, he went to New York and studied at the Art Students League. With such painters as Arshile Gorky, Willem de Kooning, and many others who have since become famous, Pollock worked on the Federal Art Project* during the depression of the 1930's. After he was included in a group show in 1940, other artists and critics wrote about his work and museums began to buy his paintings.

Although most of his financial difficulties were then over, Pollock was tortured by self-doubt and took to drinking. He continued to work, however, and he was given major museum and art gallery shows here and in Europe. In 1946 he and his wife Lee Krasner, also an artist, moved to East Hampton, Long Island, where he painted some of his most important works. In 1950 he was chosen as a representative of American art for the international exhibition called the Venice Biennale. On August 11, 1956, he died in an automobile accident.

THE WEB OF LIFE

Explaining his inventions in space and form, Jackson Pollock once said, "It seems to me that the modern painter cannot express this age, the airplane, the atom, the radio, in the old forms of the Renaissance, or of any past culture. Every age finds its own technique." But, like other great innovators in art, Pollock absorbed the inventions of earlier artists and then made his own unique contribution.

At the beginning of his career, Pollock's twisted, flame-like forms looked as if they were burning in the furnace of his emotions. In an effort to invent a picture language of his inner feelings, Pollock began to merge these violent shapes with aspects of Cubism and Symbolism, but he felt that these styles were not quite his own. Trying to liberate himself from old ways of painting, he put aside his brush and invented his famous "drip technique," using a stick dipped in paint to "pour" a picture onto the canvas. This technique allowed him complete freedom from traditional methods.

This revolutionary way of painting disturbed the art world. Many thought his techniques were merely a publicity trick. They couldn't understand that he was really creating pictures not by artful brush strokes, or the device of perspective, but by living, dynamic lines. Laid down in meshes and webs of glittering color, or sombre blacks and whites, Pollock pictured the monsters and nightmares as well as the tender lyrical spacescapes that danced across his vision.

Toward the end of his life he was hailed as a great abstract painter, implying that he painted only an abstract representation of life. Yet I believe he was painting not abstractions alone, but the space without beginning or end, with no up or down, full of cosmic energy and stardust, the space of the universe. He was painting the cosmic rhythms that rule the tides, the rising and setting sun, and our own heartbeats. That wasn't all. In his web of lines he caught the fears hidden in our minds, the joys and experiences brought to us by our senses. He painted the new regions discovered in our time—man's unconscious and the world of the atom and of space.

PORTRAIT AND A DREAM
Pollock once said: "Painting is self-discovery. Every good artist paints what he is." He invented a picture language with which he painted his inner feelings. This language may seem strange at first, but if we allow ourselves to respond with our emotions it is not difficult to understand.

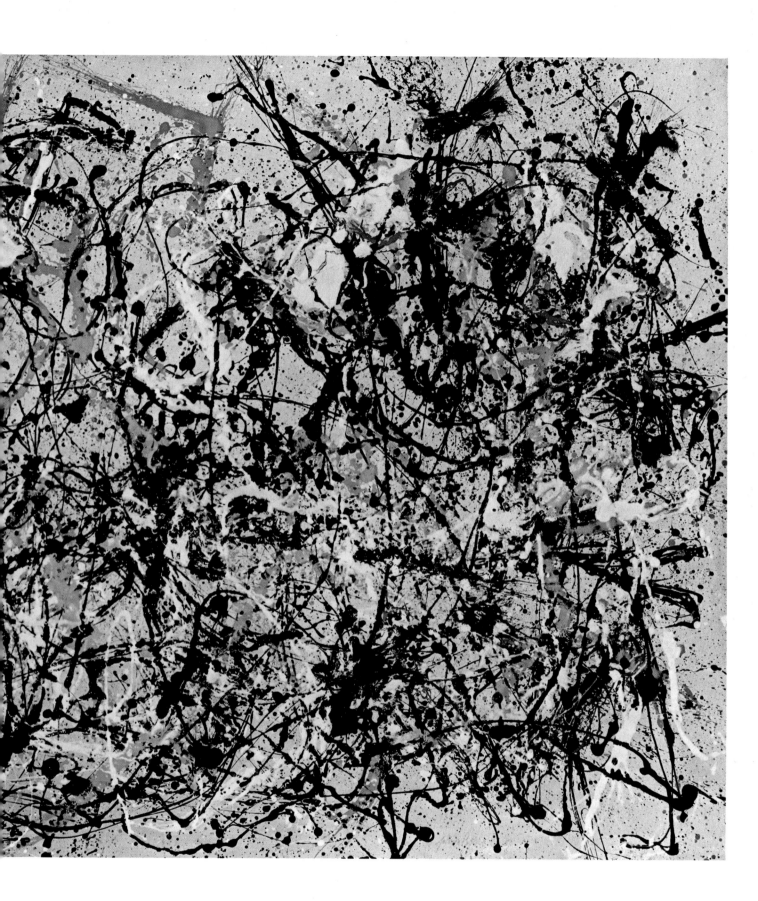

AUTUMN RHYTHM (No. 30)
Taking his cue from the Indians of Arizona and
New Mexico, who made pictures by pouring colored
sand on the ground, Pollock put his canvas on the floor
and used his painting stick like a liquid pencil in the
hands of a giant. His "drips" ended up exactly where he
wanted them. His years of practice in drawing and
painting gave him perfect control of his work.

JEAN DUBUFFET

1901—

Short, stocky and bald, Jean Dubuffet looks more like a professor than the average man's image of an artist. Born in Le Havre, France, he left his family of rich wine merchants at seventeen to live in self-enforced poverty in Paris. He attended a Paris academy of art briefly and continued his self-education by reading widely in literature, archeology and other subjects. He learned half a dozen languages and studied the accordion and the piano. Discouraged at first, he stopped painting until he discovered the art of children, primitive societies, criminals and madmen—people who seemed to him either unspoiled by civilized life or outside of the "Establishment."

After traveling abroad, Dubuffet took over his family's wine business in Paris in 1930. Drafted into World War II, he was discharged because he resisted army discipline. His first show in Paris in 1944 scandalized the French art world and several of his paintings were slashed by angry spectators. In 1946, feeling sure of his way in art, he sold his wine business. After a major exhibition of his work at the Museum of Modern Art in New York in 1962, he was hailed as the most original artist of the modern French school. He now lives with his wife in Paris and has recently become involved with music and architecture. His latest work combines architecture and art.

THE REALITY WITHIN

Jean Dubuffet distrusted all the art forms of the past. He resolved to invent a new art based on primitive feelings and visions, and made with crude matter, not old-fashioned materials like paint. The simple everyday life of common people contained more art and poetry, he felt, than famous paintings, which he found boring, make-believe and far from life. Dubuffet believes that man is not nature's highest creation, but only one form of being in the universe—like a river or a tree or the wind. Man, animals, the landscape all belong together. All life and matter are fundamentally one.

Dubuffet's aim is to return to the raw and formless. He wants to see everything fresh—as it might have been on the first day of Creation. According to Dubuffet, western civilization's idea of art and beauty is false. Distinctions between the beautiful and the ugly are nonsense. To a child, the mother who loves him is beautiful, no matter how she looks. "The beautiful," he says, "is what moves you." Dubuffet wants to invent a new language of vision based on a child's innocence and imagination. His portraits do not show what a man sees in his mirror, but what a man feels like to himself. His women have the primitive shapes of fertility goddesses and the figures in his powerful "bearded series" look like prehistoric stone idols.

Dubuffet's materials and tools are inventions too. He uses cement, tar, gravel, butterfly wings, or grass to get surprise effects and turbulent surfaces. His fingers, or spoons and knives are his tools. With these he makes his paintings look as if they are spewing out of a boiling cauldron. Always experimenting, Dubuffet paints men who look as if they were still emerging from the primeval sea slime, groping to become human. His current interest is a new kind of architectural art. In it he sculpts buildings for living or just thinking. They are inventions of the mind and try to exclude all references to nature.

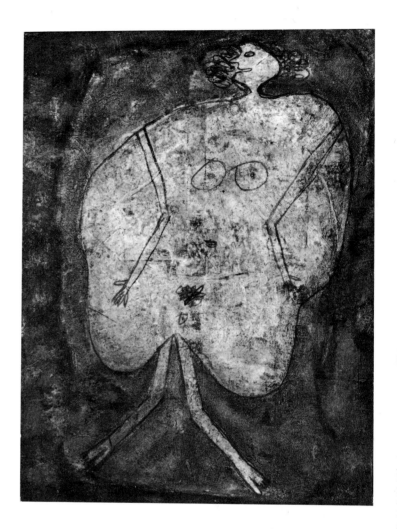

SLEEPER ON A RED BED (above)
Dubuffet tries to make us see with the innocence and imagination of a child. He succeeds in painting portraits of our primitive inner selves.

THE GEOLOGIST (left)
In this painting, as in the work of children, the space is uncertain. We see what may be a cross section of the earth's surface or it may be a view from above. The man is tiny—to show his unimportance in relation to the universe from which he came.

SUBWAY (overleaf)
In his early canvases, Dubuffet used brilliant colors. His paintings of the Paris subway are simplified by using only frontal and profile images of people. He had no respect for classic perspective and created depth by overlapping forms the way children do.

THE TRIUMPH OF COLOR

Color is the essence of painting and its chief delight. Painting is for those who are willing to plunge into a sea of color, the mysterious, exhilarating child of light. Light existed before life itself. It is the visible presence of energy. It is a force of nature that you cannot touch, smell, feel or taste. In nature, light makes color, and in art, color makes light. Adventurers in color leave the traditions of art behind and depend on their native intuition and personal observations.

Color itself has no form. The artist who uses color to convey his feelings and thoughts must create a world in which color is free—free to become space, to create depth, to suggest weight, to acquire shapes, and to convey the whole range of emotions. In the instinctive language that everyone seems to understand, red, the color of blood, is the color of life, of joy and of danger; white is the color of purity; blue of the heavenly or divine. These are the most obvious aspects of the color alphabet that artists use and that are universally recognized and enjoyed.

Ever since the days of Newton, we have known that ordinary sunlight can be broken up into the colors of the spectrum, but one of the first artists to use color to produce light was the early nineteenth-century English painter, J.M.W. Turner. In fact, when the French painters, Claude Monet and Camille Pissarro, saw Turner's work, they were so impressed that they carried on further studies of their own and helped found the Impressionist movement. The Impressionists showed that color changes with the light that is cast on it, and that changing light also changes the form of objects. This was a break with the painting of the past, which had regarded natural colors and forms as eternal.

Later, the Dutch artist Vincent Van Gogh experimented with the emotional expressiveness of color. Going beyond the idea that blue is calming, red exciting, and yellow joyful, he put into his color harmonies his impressions of evil, sin, passion, and anger.

More than ever before, in the twentieth century, artists are exploring the vast potentials of color as sources of light and pushing on to its final basic quality as light itself.

VINCENT VAN GOGH 1853–1890

**SELF-PORTRAIT
WITH PALETTE** (above)
How Van Gogh used color as a
language of feeling can be seen in this
painting. The long undulating brush
strokes create a sense of tension,
movement, excitement. The head,
moody and somber, stands out
vividly against the dark swirling
background.

CAFÉ TERRACE (right)
Familiar scenes like this one are
transformed by Van Gogh's unique
power of observation. He makes us
feel the vastness of the night sky and
the stars that seem to explode with
light. The contrast between the soft
glow from the sky and the light of
the café makes the scene more vivid
and dramatic than it could ever be
in the daytime.

Vincent Van Gogh, one of the great colorists of
modern art, came from a Dutch family of preachers,
artists, and picture dealers. When Vincent was sixteen, his father sent him to work for his uncle, an art
dealer at the Hague. Later he was transferred to
London. There the self-tortured, emotional youth
fell in love with the daughter of his landlady, the
first of many unhappy love experiences. After losing
his job at the gallery, he studied to become a preacher
but failed his examinations. This led to a nervous
breakdown but he still insisted on preaching. He
returned to Brussels, took an evangelical training
course and was finally sent to work as a missionary
among Belgian miners. Appalled by their poverty,
he gave them everything he earned, so his superiors
decided he was too impractical to hold his job.

While working among the miners, he began to
draw and paint, and his brother Theo agreed to
support him as a painter. Vincent painted everything—still lifes, peasants, miners, weavers, nature—
in the colors of coal, of earth, of darkness.

The fear of becoming ill sent him home to his
family. Restless at home, in 1887 he went to live
with his brother Theo in Paris. There he entered
art school and met such painters as Henri de
Toulouse-Lautrec and Paul Gauguin, and haunted
the Louvre Museum.

His moodiness made it impossible for him to stay
with Theo, so he moved to a small house in Arles,
in southern France, and invited Gauguin to share
it with him. But two such different men could not
get along. In a fit of rage, Van Gogh finally tried
to kill Gauguin, who fled to Paris. Deeply disturbed
by his sense of guilt, Van Gogh slashed off his ear.

No longer trusting himself to live alone, he
entered an asylum. There he remained until a
Dr. Gachet agreed to take care of him. But fits of
temper and a quarrel with Dr. Gachet drove Vincent
to desperation, and on July 27, 1890, at the age of
thirty-seven, he shot himself.

COLOR LIKE SWIRLING FLAMES

Like many of the Post-Impressionists,* as they are labelled in art history books, Van Gogh was influenced by the Japanese prints* that flooded Paris in the 1880's. He was even called the "Impressionist Japanese of Paris." Van Gogh used the flattened perspective and color effects of the prints as well as contrasts between black and white and brilliant color. Van Gogh not only understood color, as the Japanese did, for its vibrancy and its power to create form, but also for its emotional expressiveness.

During his entire life Van Gogh sold only one painting. But today there is probably no artist of the last hundred years who has a greater acceptance from millions of people everywhere.

A CAFÉ AT NIGHT (above)
Van Gogh wrote of this painting, "I have tried to
express the terrible passions of humanity by means of red
and green . . . the idea that the café is a place where
one can ruin oneself, run mad, or commit a crime, and
all this in an atmosphere like a devil's furnace, of pale
sulfur."

ROAD WITH CYPRESSES (left)
Van Gogh spoke of color in terms of feelings. He wrote
of a green "saddened by gray," and of a yellow that
"represents pure love." His colors leap and swirl as though
they were on fire, making his paintings sources
of light.

33

THE ROAD MENDERS (above)
and CHURCH AT AUVERS (right)
Van Gogh's most powerful paintings
are those of the everyday lives of the
peasants of southern France. Scenes
such as these tell us of his deep
sympathy for the people and of his
love for nature.

PAUL GAUGUIN

SELF-PORTRAIT (above)
Gauguin rejects the conventional rules
of perspective and uses flattened forms
and contrasting colors
to portray himself as a demonic
angel—complete with halo.

THE WHITE HORSE (right)
Gauguin's figures retain their natural
brown skin tones and dark hair, but
they stand out against violet trees,
blue meadows, and yellow rivers.
These visions are not copied from
nature, but are the products of a mind
saturated in color.

Paul Gauguin was a big, dark, hawk-nosed, romantic man, who boasted that he had "savage blood" in his veins. Born in Paris, he was sent as a youth to a Jesuit seminary, but left it to go to sea. Returning to Paris, Gauguin took a job with a stockbroker, married a Danish girl and had five children by her. Suddenly one day, for his own pleasure, he began to paint. Then, at thirty-five, apparently fed up with his middle-class existence, Gauguin resigned from the stockbroker's office, left his family, and devoted himself to painting.

Still dissatisfied with his life, and yearning to see exotic places, Gauguin shipped out for Martinique in the Caribbean, but his health broke down and he had to work his way back to France. In 1888 he had his first one-man show and visited Van Gogh in Arles. But when Van Gogh, in a fit of insanity, threatened to kill him, Gauguin left for Paris.

Unable to make a living from his painting, he decided to abandon France and civilization, and in 1891 sailed for Tahiti. The primitive rites of the Tahitians, the beauty of the girls, the magnificent scenery enchanted him. "Here, near my cabin," he wrote, "I dream of violent harmonies, enhanced by I know not what sacred horror." Despite his fascination, he went back to Brittany, but again had no success with his paintings. He had a second exhibit of his works in Paris and again returned to Tahiti.

From there he later wrote a friend: "My health falls off every day." Then, financial problems and, finally, the death of his favorite daughter in Paris plunged him into despair. He tried to commit suicide. He survived, but misfortune followed him everywhere. In 1903 he was sentenced to jail for writing an abusive letter to a local official but died before he could serve his sentence.

A PARADISE OF COLOR

Gauguin's contribution to art was more than a vision of the exotic beauty of Tahiti, the native girls, and the tropical forest. His almost harsh color combinations, his flattened forms and his sharp

contrasts, prepared the way for a group of rebellious painters called the "Fauves,"*meaning Wild Beasts. They believed that painting was primarily the art of using color.

Gauguin blended blues and reds so that they seem to force each other into greater brightness. He combined greens and blacks and browns, which usually give a muddy look to paintings, and made them radiant by touching them with iridescent reds. His colors often form abstractions, so that one feels that with one more step he would have become an abstract painter.

Gauguin recognized his role as a great liberator. He said, "I tried to establish the right to draw anything, and the painters who are now enjoying this liberty owe something to me." He gave us, in the end, a paradise of color.

THE SORCERER (right) and
THE DEAD WATCHING (below)
Gauguin was fascinated with the primitive rites of the Tahitians, and often used them as subject matter for his paintings.

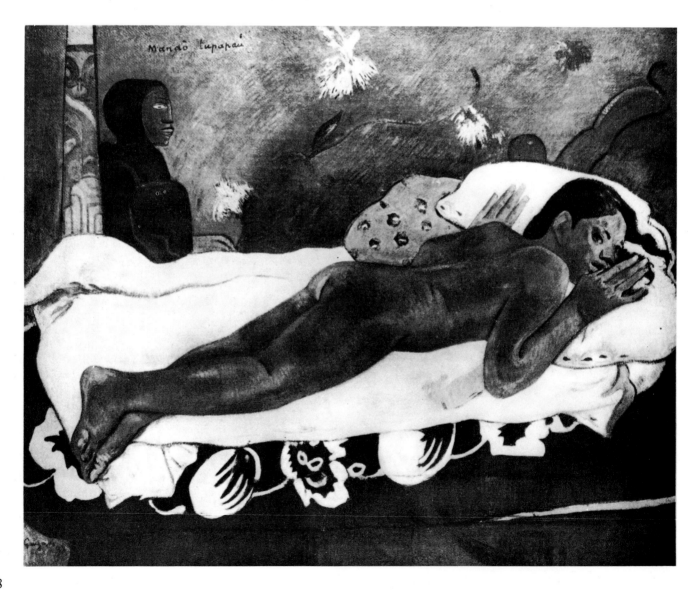

TAHITIAN WOMEN WITH
MANGOES (left) and
TWO WOMEN ON
THE BEACH (above)
In these paintings Gauguin clearly
expresses his enchantment with the
lush beauty and natural way of life
of the Tahitian women.

HENRI MATISSE

1869—1955

SEATED BLUE NUDE,
NO. 4 (above)
Shortly before his death, Matisse did
a series of extremely simplified
female figures composed of cut-and-
pasted paper. Using scissors, as he
had once used a pen or brush,
he drew forms on blue paper and
pasted them on a white background.

PARK IN TANGIER (left)
Learning from Cézanne and Van Gogh,
Matisse abandoned shadows, discarded
classic perspective, and used color
alone, without any outline, to create
form. A visit to Tangier intensified
his interest in color and tropical
foliage.

Henri Matisse was born in the north of France. His
father, a wealthy merchant, hoped that his son would
study law, and young Henri entered the University of
Paris. But after copying a lithograph when he was about
twenty, Matisse knew that painting was the only career
for him. He said, "I felt transported into a paradise in
which I was gloriously free."

His father finally allowed him to study painting with
Bouguereau, then the most successful painter in Paris.
When Matisse saw the photographic quality of that
painter's work, he despaired of becoming an artist, and
his teacher discouraged him, saying, "You'll never learn
to draw." He was about to give up art when he came
upon the last, loosely painted, almost impressionistic
work of the great Spanish painter, Goya. "I can paint
like that," he said, and went back to his studies. Later,
rejecting Bouguereau's standards, he said, "Exactitude is
not truth."

An artist in those days was regarded as an outcast who
broke all rules of behavior. Matisse, however, promised
his father he would be a conventional, well-behaved
family man. He was, all his life—except in his art.

In 1905, Matisse became the leader of a group of artists
who wanted to break the back of classic art, and maintained that faces could be green or violet, that water
could be red, that perspective was old-fashioned and
classic art finished. They were attacked by the critics and
called the "Fauves," that is, Wild Beasts.

At the famous Armory Show in New York in 1913,
the first major exhibition of European painting in the
United States, Matisse's work was again attacked, and it
wasn't until 1927, when he won first prize at an international exhibition in Pittsburgh, that he was recognized
as one of the great masters of painting.

In 1931, Matisse was commissioned to decorate the
large hall of the Barnes Museum at Merion, Pennsylvania.
It turned out to be one of his masterpieces. In 1949, he
designed the Chapel at Vence in France, including the
altar, the dress and the religious paintings, a project which
he considered his greatest work. His fame was surpassed
only by his lifelong friend, the Spanish-French painter,
Picasso. Matisse died of a heart attack at the age of 85.

LOVER OF LIGHT

Almost from the start, Matisse was fascinated by color. Although his first paintings were in the somber browns and grays popular at that time, he soon began to use bright colors and by 1898 he painted a male nude, not in flesh tones but entirely in blue, breaking all the traditions of art.

He noticed as he worked how much light seemed to come from the contrasts of pure bright colors. He observed that Cézanne was able to suggest the near and far by colors alone, and, looking at Van Gogh's work, he became aware that emotions could be expressed through violent contrasting hues. A magician of color, he created harmonies and contrasts that few earlier painters had dared use.

Matisse did not pour on paint as many modern artists do. He preferred light, transparent color effects, and his canvases would sometimes look like watercolors.* Working with a brush and a rag full of turpentine, which thins out color, he would fill in with the brush and rub out with the rag. He kept at it until he got the exact form and color he wanted, directly, without overpainting. The most difficult task was getting the wild color and spontaneous forms he was after. He said, "Order above all in color. Put three or four touches of color that you have understood upon the canvas; add another if you can. If you cannot, set this canvas aside and begin again." Towards the end of his life, he said, "What I dream of is an art of balance, of purity, of serenity, devoid of all depressive subject matter; an art that is an appeasing influence, like a good armchair in which to rest." Matisse's paintings, full of light and joy, great outbursts of color, are witnesses to his success.

After a lifetime of working with color as a source of light, when questioned as to what would be the next stage in painting, he answered, "Light."

THE PURPLE ROBE
Matisse dreamed of making his pictures gay and sensuous, spontaneous and free, but he planned them as carefully as a scientist. Experimenting with line and color, he combined stripes and curved lines with arabesque* and floral patterns to create bold compositions.

SOUVENIR OF OCEANIA (left) and BLUE NUDE, THE FROG (above)

Toward the end of his life Matisse became an invalid and partially blind, but he went on working from his bed with scissors, colored paper and glue, making collages—some of the most delightful and joyous works of his career. A few of these compositions (left) came closer to being complete abstractions than any of his earlier work. Thus the upper section of the figure above consists of three almost identical circles inside the uplifted arms.

HANS HOFMANN

1880—1967

If German-born Hans Hofmann had had a better sense of business, he would probably never have been an artist. As a young boy he visited his grandfather's farm along a barge canal; there he studied the changing reflections of trees and houses in the water, and he began to wonder which was more real.

Although interested in art from the very beginning, he became a science student to please his father. He also learned to play the violin and the organ, and later transferred his feelings for rhythm, intervals and tone into paint. At sixteen he broke with his father and took a job with the Director of Public Works in Munich. There he began to study engineering, and soon invented an electromagnetic comptometer. His father, thinking Hans would now become an engineer, gave him a thousand gold marks, a large sum in those days. Young Hans promptly left his job, registered in art school and got married. He continued to pour out inventions, but they were unprofitable because he was a poor businessman. Finally, he gave up engineering and devoted himself to art. A rich man became interested in his work and helped him to go to Paris to study art.

At the outbreak of World War I, he had to leave Paris. Back in Munich, he opened an art school, and before long students from all over the world were coming to him. He was invited to teach at the University of California in 1930. Then, with Hitler's rise to power, he settled permanently in the United States. By 1934 he had founded his own school in New York and on Cape Cod. During the last decade of his life he devoted himself entirely to painting, establishing himself at the ripe age of sixty-five as a leader of the new Abstract Expressionist* movement. He continued painting into his eighties. In 1969, the Metropolitan Museum of Art in New York chose him as one of the painters who changed the course of American art.

"I LOVE TO SWIM IN COLOR"

Smiling broadly, his jolly face lit up as if he had turned on a switch inside, Hans Hofmann would say in his thick Bavarian accent, "I love to swim in color," and this was apparent in everything he did. Color determines form, he believed. We must discard old-fashioned perspective in which objects are shown in diminishing scale, the further they are from the viewer. Space must be created by form and color relationships. These relationships push and pull against each other on the surface of the canvas, creating dynamic energy. This energy becomes the life of the picture.

These ideas agreed with discoveries by scientists that space is full of energy, that it has no beginning or end, no up or down. Hofmann also believed that the goal of painting is to reveal the relationship between objects and their basic unity, not to emphasize their differences. Painting, moreover, is not based on visual perceptions alone. "We see with all our senses; all our senses are dependent on each other," he said. "In the mind they join and overlap." Feeling was another way to know reality. By combining the evidence of his senses with his experiences and emotions, the artist can achieve the vital force of nature itself. This inner vision, using hearing and touch as well as the sense of space and movement, shows all through his work.

THE CONJURER

According to Hofmann, it is the color development of a painting that determines the form. He believed that the affect of a color is entirely dependent on its relation to other colors. Colors can create their own space by the vibrancy of their light.

48

AUTUMN CHILL AND SUN
Hofmann's art is among the most
radical experiments in modern art.
His bold use of color and his total
liberation of it, to the point of having
no subject matter except color itself,
make him a pioneer of what is known
as "Abstract Expressionism."

PAINTERS WHO FREED THEIR EMOTIONS

The Spartan who hid his emotions was long regarded as the masculine ideal. Even today we consider it bad taste to show too much emotion, and men especially are supposed to hide what they feel. But we have learned that feelings too long stifled may explode.

Even before most of us realized this, certain modern artists decided to paint the world of inner feelings. The outside world no longer interested them. They were not content to portray love with pictures of lovers kissing, or sadness with a mother mourning her child. Just as we recognize a smile as a sign of happiness, and tears as the mark of sorrow, artists searched for a language of feeling, a pictorial code so vivid and powerful that it would be understood by everyone. They called on every imaginative device to convey the strongest emotions. Distorted forms, convulsive lines and raw colors, were applied to objects, landscapes and portraits alike. What the artist of the emotions finally shows us is not what he sees, but what he feels about what he sees.

EDVARD MUNCH

1863–1944

THE CRY (above)
In one of the most dramatic examples of his picture writing, Munch makes us experience the terror of a girl caught in the grip of something beyond her control. The contrasting straight diagonal lines and curves make the painting seem to move in several directions at once, emphasizing conflicting emotions and heightening the nightmarish effect.

GIRLS ON THE BRIDGE (right)
Although Munch usually portrayed women as monsters bent on destroying men, he occasionally painted young girls with charm and understanding.

Edvard Munch decided to become an artist when he was seventeen years old. The emphasis on death and sickness which marked his work from the beginning sprang from the fact that his mother died of tuberculosis when he was five, and his sisters later died from the same disease. As a youth he studied at the School of Design in Oslo, Norway. He went to Paris for the first time in 1885. The modern paintings he saw there, and particularly the work of the Impressionists, were among the great influences on his art.

In 1892 he was given a show in Berlin which aroused such violent protest that it was forced to close after one week. This, however, gave him international publicity and he went on to show his work in Germany, Scandinavia and Holland. In 1895 his famous lithograph *The Cry* appeared. Despite his growing success, he had a nervous breakdown and spent six months in a hospital. Later, he settled in a small town outside Oslo, where he continued to paint for the rest of his life. During the Hitler regime in Germany, the Nazis branded his works as degenerate and confiscated them. He was very prolific and when he died in 1944 he left one thousand paintings, fifteen thousand prints, 4400 watercolors and drawings, and six sculptures to the City of Oslo.

SUFFERING REVEALED

Edvard Munch tried to express his inner feelings, and especially loneliness, fear, and suffering, by means of distorted forms and intense colors. He would often resort to grotesque caricature and satire to sharpen his effects. After the death of his mother and two sisters, death and illness was his subject all his life. He also viewed sexual love as a threat and he portrayed women as demons, vampires and ruthless goddesses of fertility who attract men only to destroy them. This "anti-woman" attitude was made popular at the turn of the century by various European writers. Paintings

GALLOPING HORSE (above)
The huge horse in this painting almost fills the foreground.
The onlookers and the snowy landscape are just a
stage-set through which the animal plunges madly,
unrestrained by man, who is barely visible.

MELANCHOLIA (left, above)
This is a painting of a hallucination—how a room looks
to a depressed woman. The lines of the room curve and
meet each other and the vivid oranges and yellows are
like fleeting flames. The dark eyes of the woman, who
sits motionless and drained of energy, staring inward, are
the only fixed points in the painting.

THE DANCE OF LIFE (left, below)
The contrasts which appear over and over in Munch's
paintings—life and death, darkness and light—dominate
this picture. Life, symbolized by the young girl in white
(left) and the somber figure of death (right) stand over
the central figures, who move as though in a trance while
the other dancers whirl madly around.

like *The Vampire, Madonna, The Beast,* are typical
expressions of this feeling.

While in Paris, he came under the influence of
Gauguin, Toulouse-Lautrec and the Impressionists,
and for a time painted gay street scenes of life in
Paris and Oslo. But this light mood was brief. He
soon returned to his own emotional language, in
which his figures and landscapes seem bound together in suffering. In his great mural, *Frieze of
Life,* which he worked on all through his career,
he tried to paint Life, Love and Death and to show
that suffering and joy could be united with the
forces of nature. Here his landscapes become symbols
of simple beauty, no longer objects of terror.

Later Munch painted a mural* for the University
of Oslo in which the sun is the center, symbol of
life and light. After this mural Munch's colors
became almost as brilliant as those of the Fauves.
But toward the end of his life he returned to the
wildness of Nature.

Munch's work defies analysis because no matter
what simple scene or figure he paints or etches—two
women sitting in the open, or himself in a room
between a bed and a clock—the settings are cells
of isolation, leaving us waiting in suspense for the
outer mask to fall off and reveal the inner despair.

Munch influenced not only such men of his own
period as Soutine and Kirchner but even the artists
of today who are still seeking to express, visually,
man's hidden feelings of loneliness, fear and despair.

CHAIM SOUTINE

1894–1943

SELF-PORTRAIT
Soutine was a slight, handsome man with intense
dark eyes, a charming smile and elegant hands. But
he painted himself with thick lips, tiny eyes and coarse
features. His low opinion of himself came partly
from his tragic childhood.

Tenth of eleven children of a poor tailor, Chaim
Soutine was born in a Polish village. He knew
only poverty, starvation and cruelty as a child.
At thirteen, when he began to draw on scraps
of paper he tore from the wall, his brothers
beat him unmercifully because the Jewish faith
forbids the making of images.

He left home at sixteen to study art at Minsk,
Poland, and he became a brilliant student. In 1913

he went to Paris and while attending art school
worked as a porter and a ditch digger to keep alive.
In doing so he ruined his health and crippled himself
emotionally. In 1918 he left Paris and went to
southern France where he lived and worked for
three years. A rich man's support made it possible
for him to paint a series of canvases which won
him delayed fame. When in 1923 Albert C. Barnes,
the famous American collector, bought about one
hundred of his paintings, Soutine's money worries
were over. During World War II when the Nazis
occupied most of France, he was forced into hiding.
He died while undergoing an operation in August,
1943.

THE TORTURED SPIRIT

In the village where Soutine was born, violent
emotions, intense excitement and demonic energy
were the only escape for the Jewish community
from the pressures of poverty and persecution. This
atmosphere of turmoil left its mark on the art of
Soutine. Violence, suffering and murder were his
subject matter. Soutine did not treat these subjects
calmly and objectively. He painted them as if he
himself were the tortured tree form, the starved
and frightened child, the murdered dog. It was as
though he got inside his subject matter, into every
aspect of it. The paintings became both an accusation
and a punishment. "This is what men do," he
seemed to say. "Look—and suffer. I did."

Early in life he studied such masters as El Greco
and Rembrandt, who were also concerned with
man's agony. His world was a grotesque one of
anguish with overtones of grim comedy—as if the
sufferings of men and their callous cruelty were
comic to the gods. Few artists in history have
painted suffering humanity as boldly and power-
fully as he did.

PAGE BOY AT MAXIM'S

In this cartoon-like figure of a bellboy holding out his hand for a tip, we can see the anguish, tinged with comedy, of Soutine's world. Using a sinuous line charged with vibrant force, and heavily painted surfaces in wild colors, Soutine projected his tortured feelings with the directness of a cry of pain.

ERNST LUDWIG KIRCHNER

1880–1938

German-born Ernst Ludwig Kirchner was largely self-taught, first studying architecture and then turning to painting. The work of Munch, the native art of the South Sea islands, and primitive African sculptures, as well as crude old German woodcuts,* had a deep influence on him.

Moving to Dresden, he became the leader of a group of artists who called themselves "DieBrücke" (The Bridge) because they hoped through their art to show the way to the future. The group split up about 1911 and Kirchner continued developing his unique style, producing an astonishing variety of work in every medium.*

Assigned to artillery during World War I, he could not adjust to army life and had a severe nervous breakdown. After the war he went to live in Switzerland, where he fell ill with tuberculosis. This, together with the confiscation of his paintings by the Nazi government and the growing power of Hitler, plunged him into such a deep depression that he committed suicide.

THE LONELY CROWD

Long before we realized that an individual in a crowd can be just as lonely as an individual in the wilderness, Ernst Kirchner was painting the inhabitants of modern cities, their closed-off existence and their tragic loneliness. Aware of the suffering of such people around him, he strove to revive emotion in art and he dared to do what few artists had done before him—paint human feelings.

Trying to make his emotional messages easy to grasp, he set down the hurdy-gurdy life of the music halls and circuses in raw neon-light colors and harsh forms to give his viewers an emotional jolt. As one of the leaders of the group known as "The Bridge," he told of their break with the past: "As a young band and as bearers of the future, we seek the freedom to work and live as

against the older established powers"—the kind of statement that might be made by many young people today. A student of Cubism, he painted figures and scenes as viewed from several angles at the same time.

Settling in Switzerland after World War I, Kirchner was inspired by the simple lives of the peasants and the splendor of the mountains to paint his most lyrical works. In the Alps, he felt that man and nature were at last in harmony.

Searching all his life to put down in picture writing man's deepest feelings, he skillfully peeled off the surface of sophisticated society to show the emptiness behind the gaudy facade.

SEATED WOMAN
"My goal," Kirchner said, "was always to express emotion and experience with large, simple forms and clear colors." Here he uses the geometric forms of the Cubists and brilliant colors of the Fauves to do just that.

THE STREET

It was in his Berlin street scenes that Kirchner was most
successful in portraying the "lonely crowd." The
desperate nightly parade of pleasure-seeking men and
women, each one shut into his isolated, mechanized life,
appear as animated puppets, not human beings.

WILLEM DE KOONING 1904—

In 1924, at twenty-one, Willem de Kooning, a penniless stowaway from his native Rotterdam, landed in New York. While an art student, he worked as a house painter and also did some commercial art. Somehow he managed to get along and make friends with some of the best artists of the time. Uncertain about his talents, de Kooning turned down many chances to exhibit his work and he rarely sold his paintings.

It was not until 1948 that he had his first one-man exhibition. Nothing was sold. But in 1953 a showing of his "Women" series established him as a leading Abstract Expressionist. Even in the late 1950's he declined a show at the Museum of Modern Art in New York, saying, "I'm not ready. I'm still working out of doubt." Finally in 1969 he agreed to an exhibition of his major works at the Museum of Modern Art, but he disliked the idea, declaring, "A retrospective show is like being tied up like a sausage and stamped 'Finished.'" But de Kooning

WOMAN, I (right)
De Kooning's woman is not like any who ever lived. She is a goddess of death, with sawteeth, mad eyes and bloated body—portrait of a ruthless society that devours its children. She is also a landscape, savage sex and mindless power. "She has nothing to do with women," says de Kooning. "I'm afraid of her myself."

DOOR TO THE RIVER
(far right)
When the women began to disappear from de Kooning's canvases he replaced them with abstract landscapes. His forms became larger and more simple and his colors cleaner and more intense. He used greens, yellows, blues, browns—the colors of grass, beach, sky and earth. The painting becomes a pattern from which we can experience any number of emotions. What you get from it depends partially on your own personality and imagination.

SEATED WOMAN
In this early painting de Kooning's shapes still bear a strong likeness to reality, but we can see the beginning of his gradual development toward complete abstraction.

certainly was not finished. The exhibition went to Amsterdam and increased his international reputation.

Now in his sixties, silver-haired, blue-eyed, with the lean, clear look of a poet, Willem de Kooning is a gentle, jovial man who charms everyone. In the past, the dark side of his nature often plunged him into despair, but in recent years his work has changed. In his enormous studio on Long Island, his paintings have become celebrations of joy, success and the delights of living—and painting.

NEW LANGUAGE OF FEELING

Willem de Kooning is an Abstract Expressionist. The original Expressionists such as Munch, Kirchner and Soutine (see Chapter 3) depended on familiar subjects to convey their feelings—a screaming girl to depict terror, writhing landscapes to suggest suffering, angular figures to show despair and loneliness. To set the emotional tone of their images they used colors that were harsh and moody.

De Kooning wanted to find a way to paint feelings without using human figures or familiar objects. Like all abstractionists, he made use of simple psychological facts that we all understand. We know from experience that sharp angular objects are painful to touch, curves are pleasing, horizontal lines suggest rest, diagonal lines suggest movement, and so on. We also generally agree that red, the color of blood, is exciting and that blue, the color of sky, is calming. Building on such emotionally charged symbols and colors, de Kooning developed a huge vocabulary of images for making Abstract Expressionist paintings.

Imaginative forms in endless variety flowed from his brush. He created shapes that were voluptuous, cruel, soothing, joyful. He made shapes that seemed to move, and some that were as still as stones; happy shapes and tragic ones. He made colors that could say love or joy as tenderly as a kiss and colors that told of anger and misery as clearly as a cry. De Kooning made his paintings speak to our intuitions and our unconscious minds in symbols that we can understand if we use our feelings and intuitions as well as our reason.

DREAMS AND NIGHTMARES

In the early part of the twentieth century the great Viennese psychiatrist Sigmund Freud introduced us to the power of our unconscious mind. He helped us see that reason is only a thin layer over the seething volcano of human desires, angers and fears hidden in our unconscious.

Artists and poets have always been aware of this. From Bosch to Goya, from the ancient Greeks to Shakespeare, they have told us about the monsters and the beauties of this unknown region. During the 1920's artists everywhere began to explore this boundless area where life and death, the past and future, the real and the imaginary are united. They felt that the inner world of man was just as real as the outside world and should be revealed. They found that seemingly unrelated things have deep connections that we all understand. Who needs to be told what skulls, deserts and crutches symbolize? Or lovers, flowers, the sun or birds? In the world of the imagination, limp watches have faces like men, goats become princes who play the violin, and men in bowler hats fall from the sky like rain.

If much of this seems like nonsense, that is how it strikes the artist. Artists learned long ago what scientists only recently discovered—that nonsense comes closer to our unconscious than common sense, and reveals more clearly those mysterious forces that seem to govern man's behavior.

MARC CHAGALL

1887—

Perhaps Marc Chagall became a master of fantasy, the poetry of romantic love, and intense emotional color because he lived through some of our time's most agonizing crises.

The son of a poor Jewish fish-merchant, Chagall was born in Vitebsk, a small city in Russia. Life in the Jewish ghetto was a major influence on him. He first studied with a local portrait painter, then in Paris and Berlin. Returning to Russia in 1915, he founded an academy of art in Vitebsk. But he soon came into conflict with various factions and left Russia for France. His first one-man exhibition in Paris, in 1924, was full of memories of his Russian childhood. His reputation grew and at the 1939 Carnegie exhibition in Pittsburgh, he won first prize.

Distressed with the growing political unrest in Europe, Chagall moved to the United States in 1941. There he completed the set for Igor Stravinsky's famous ballet, *Firebird*. When World War II was over he went to live in France. Interested in all the art media, he illustrated a number of classic books, designed stained glass windows for a synagogue in Jerusalem and for a church near Tarrytown, New York, and finished a large mural for New York City's new Metropolitan Opera House. Now in his eighties, a stocky man with wild curly hair, he happily continues to turn out ceramics, etchings and lyrical paintings from his home in Vence, France.

DREAMS OF LOVE AND SORROW

Marc Chagall's dream world springs from Jewish and Russian folk tales, from the Bible, popular superstitions, miracle-making rabbis, and the customs of his native Russian town. "Our whole inner world is reality," he said, "perhaps even more real than the apparent world."

Love, death and suffering are his recurring themes, but love most of all. His lovers are among the most tender in art history. They appear entwined in a bouquet of flowers, flying on a fairy-tale horse, kissing as they float over Paris, the Venus of cities. The dream and the reality become one, the miracle becomes truth, and the world is a happy place. While his art owes much to French artists who explored the geometry of forms and emotional color, Chagall transformed these qualities into a language in which he speaks to the whole world with the clarity and innocence of a child and the wisdom of a master.

I AND MY VILLAGE
Chagall uses the devices of Cubism to create a world of dreams and fantasy from the memories of his native Russian town.

64

THE FIREBIRD (a curtain design, above)
and THE JUGGLER (right)
Other painters released their feelings
in distorted forms and lines and
played with double images, but
Chagall outdid them all. He made
his subjects transparent, painted x-ray
views of cows, put wings on clocks,
and mocked the laws of gravity.

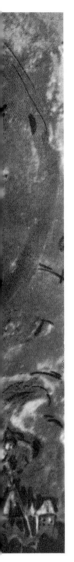

DOUBLE PORTRAIT WITH
A GLASS OF WINE (left) and
HALF-PAST THREE (right)
On Chagall's canvases, done in
incandescent colors and wild folk
imagery, anything can happen. His
vision is like ours, only more
sensuous and exalted. In his dreams,
people become animals and
cows carry umbrellas, play violins,
and parade as lovers.

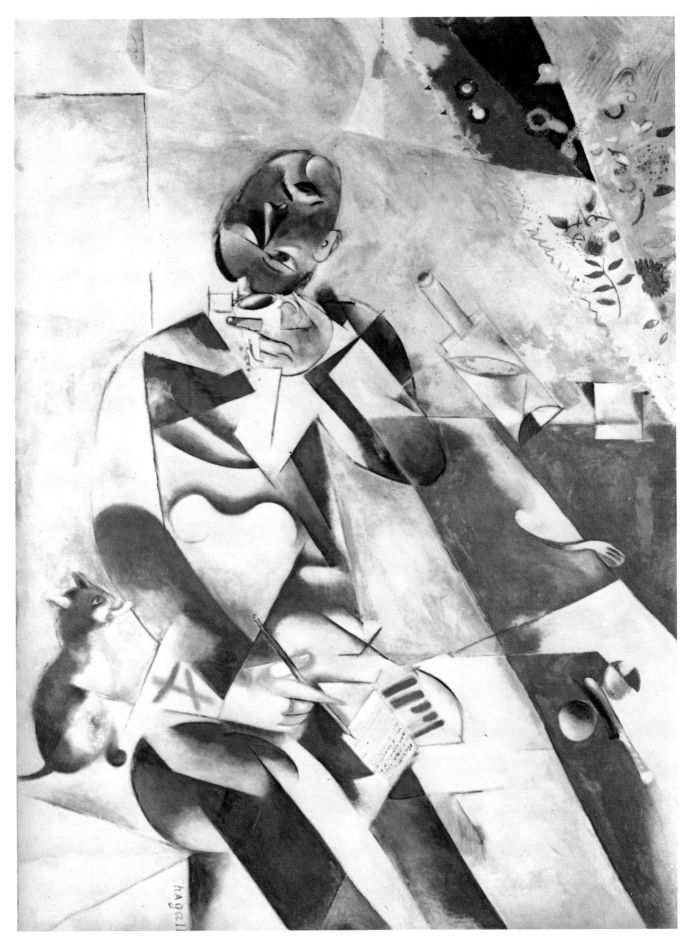

SALVADOR DALI

1904—

By the time he was thirty, Salvador Dali had created enough scandals and legends to last another man a lifetime. Born in Figueras, Spain, he had completed two huge oil paintings in the traditional style before he was ten. Later, at the National Art Academy in Madrid, he won many prizes and became a master of technique. In 1924 he was briefly jailed for anti-government activity and finally expelled from school. That year he was given his first one-man show in Madrid.

Settling in Paris in 1928, he joined the group of artists who were exploring the subconscious. Because they went beneath the "realistic" surface of life they were called "Surrealists." In 1931 he painted *The Persistence of Memory*, which created a furor with its limp watches in a vast desert-like expanse. In 1941 the Museum of Modern Art in New York gave him a major exhibition. While in New York he was accused of being a publicity hunter when he crashed through a Fifth Avenue window to rearrange a display of his that had been changed. In 1949 he did a number of religious paintings in the traditional manner for the Catholic Church.

One of the most versatile artists of our time, Dali was not only a pioneer in recording the nightmares that come out of the subconscious, but he designed furniture, jewelry, and even clothes, created sets for ballets and plays, and wrote movie scripts, a book of poems, and a novel.

Dali is a small, dark man with an intense face, penetrating eyes, and an exaggerated waxed moustache. He has said of himself: "The only difference between me and a madman is that I am not mad."

HALLUCINATIONS BECOME REAL

As a young art student Dali already had a reputation for fantastic behavior. When told to copy a

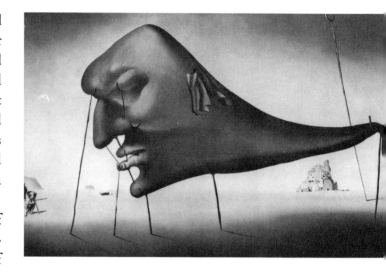

SLUMBER (above) and BURNING GIRAFFE (right) Dali has constantly shown objects, animals, and men as limp, without backbones, and needing to be propped up with crutches. In visions such as these he painted not the outside world, but his feelings of disintegration, of time passing, and of man's surrender to the machine.

Gothic madonna, he painted a pair of scales, declaring, "You may see the Virgin, but I see a pair of scales." Later, explaining his rebellious imagination, Dali claimed that all art springs from "hallucinatory" energy. He credited his visions to a special sensitivity that enabled him to see in all objects meanings hidden from normal beings.

In another famous statement he declared, "I hate simplicity in all its forms," thereby rejecting Cubism and abstract art, which seemed to him a dead end. He himself became obsessed with the possibilities of painting movement and combining different views of an object. But he also studied the works of old masters like Vermeer and Raphael and achieved a striking precision of style. An eccentric but genuine pioneer, Dali's message has yet to be fully understood.

THE PERSISTENCE OF
MEMORY (above) and
ACCOMMODATIONS
OF DESIRE (right)
A leader in the movement to explore
man's nightmares and dreams, Dali
painted with a precise realism so that
his fearsome visions would be accepted
as real. His world is a frightening one
where nothing is certain except
destruction and decay.

PAUL KLEE

Born near Berne, Switzerland, the son of a music teacher, Paul Klee loved art and music almost equally. He went to a local art school and later the Munich Art Academy. Settling in Munich in 1906, he married a pianist. There he quickly made friends with such artists as Kandinsky and Franz Marc and helped to found the "Blue Rider" group, artists who were interested in expressing emotions in raw color. Then a trip to Tunisia changed his life and strongly influenced his art. The brilliant sunshine, the exotic mosques and minarets, and the Arab tribesmen in their colorful dress enthralled him.

In 1918, after a brief stay in the army, he went back to Munich where his works were exhibited. He also had a successful career as a teacher at the Bauhaus, a new and advanced school there. Although he did not consider himself a Surrealist, he was included in the Surrealist Exhibition in Paris in 1925. He traveled in Sicily, southern France and Egypt,

and traces of all these places appear in his work. When the Nazis came to power in Germany, he was dismissed from the Bauhaus because his work was considered degenerate. He returned to Switzerland. Exhibitions of his work in Paris, London and New York brought him fame before he died.

SPONTANEOUS FANTASY

Forerunner of the Surrealists, Paul Klee translated into visual images the phantoms and strange visions that appear in our dreams and nightmares. The wild energies of our unconscious were his subjects. He felt that dreams as well as portraits or still lifes deserved to be painted. In watercolor, etching,* drawings and oils, Klee worked to make visible the invisible, to bring man face to face with his unknown inner life.

His work resembles that of children and primitive people who still retain their spontaneity. Like them he drew on deep springs that come from no one knows where. He said that, like the trunk of a tree, he only gathered and passed on what came to him from the depths. Klee's depths were deeper and more refined than those of children or primitive people, but his dependence on his roots was the same as theirs. So he made landscapes with musical notes as trees, twittering machines as singing birds, and suns as balloons. He dreamed up cities of wonder with glittering towers entered by mysterious paths through hidden gates.

DEATH AND FIRE (left)
Using black-magic symbols, Klee drew the fright of a child, not the child; the playfulness of a cat, not the cat; the feeling of death, not death.

PUPPET THEATER (right)
Klee's images seem childlike, but they are symbols of a very precise language which he created to express his fantasies and dreams. He explored the depths of his imagination to give us visual "fairy tales" like this one.

"Penetrating vision and depth of feeling are more important than appearance," he tells us. Man, not as he is, but as he might be, fascinated him. The process of becoming was more important to him than the final form of things. But he always insisted that we dream our own fairy tales into existence, that his paintings were only the start of a journey into ourselves where there are wonders beyond our wildest imaginings.

FISH MAGIC (above)
Here Klee creates a playground in which clowns, fishes and flowers, stars and suns float together under a dark moon.

ARAB SONG (right)
Klee was dramatically influenced by a trip to Egypt, after which he wrote, "I am possessed by color. I do not need to pursue it. I and color are one. I am a painter."

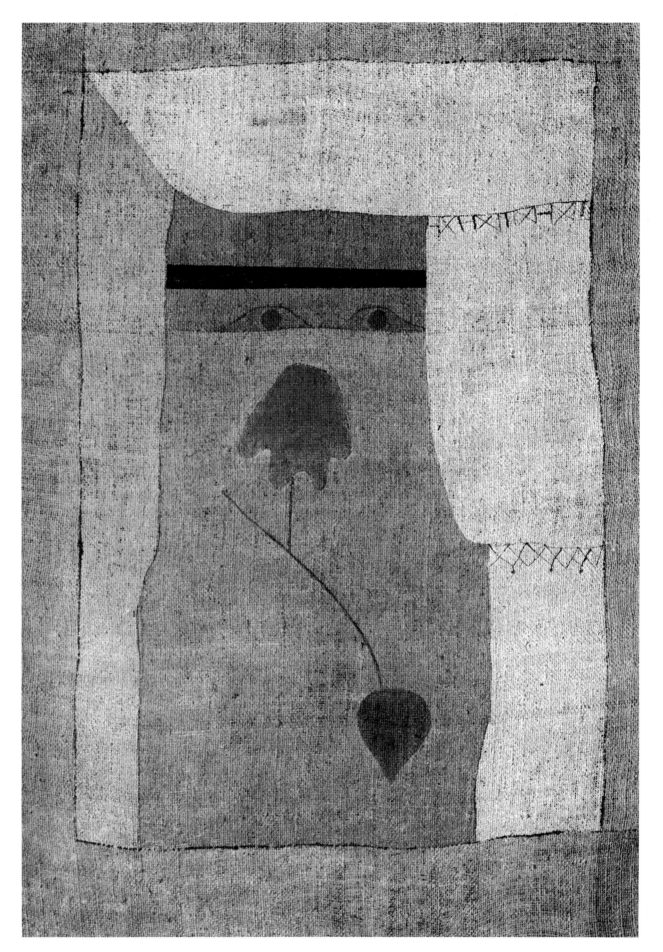

TREE RHYTHM (left)
Combining his love for art and music, Klee arranges trees in a striped landscape like notes in the musical staff. He translates the rhythm and pulse-beat of nature into visual images.

SENECIO (below)
Klee was fascinated by what man might be rather than what he is. He peopled his universe with whimsical creatures and spirits of the earth, sea and air.

RENÉ MAGRITTE

1898—1969

René Magritte was the son of a Belgian business-man. He grew up to be a kind and gentle man who looked like a business executive, talked like a scientist, and thought like a poet. A very witty man of average height, he had gray eyes and a large, round, reflective face. Nobody would have guessed that he was one of the great painters of dreams.

As a child of seven, he was astonished to see a grown man painting. He thought that only children painted. At twelve he resolved to become an artist and promptly joined a painting and sketching class. The suicide of his mother, when he was fourteen, shocked him deeply and probably helps to explain his macabre imagination. Later, he studied at the Brussels Academy, where he learned to paint objects with vivid realism.

He joined a group of Belgian artists who were interested in painting fantasies and dreams, but when his first show was reviewed unfavorably, he left Belgium for Paris. Returning after a few years, he lived modestly with his wife and dogs, played chess and the piano, read detective stories and went to the movies. He visited the United States in 1965, when his works were exhibited at the Museum of Modern Art in New York. Because recognition of his work came so late in his own country, he refused the title of Baron when it was offered to him by the King.

THE COMMONPLACE AS MAGIC

Magritte painted the commonplace that others find boring because it has become familiar. He forces us to re-examine everyday things and to consider them outside of their usual setting. A huge granite boulder is ordinary enough—but not when it floats in a blue sky. A locomotive on a track hardly attracts attention, but suppose you saw it suddenly burst into a living room. At every turn he transforms ordinary things into their opposites. Shoes become feet, a fish ends with a woman's legs. Even the landscape is not safe from him. He does paintings within paintings to mix illusion and reality.

By joining unrelated, far-fetched and strange objects, Magritte blasts our minds open to feelings and ideas for which we have, so far, neither the words nor even an alphabet.

THE FALSE MIRROR (left, above), THE LISTENING
CHAMBER (left) and PERSONAL VALUES (above)
Magritte gives us something like the magic mushroom
eaten by Alice in Wonderland that made her grow as
tall as a tree. What could be more commonplace than an
apple? Except when Magritte makes it occupy a whole
room. An eyeball becomes a huge window through
which we see clouds floating in a blue sky. The comb,
glass, matchstick and shaving brush in a room (above)
are certainly familiar enough, except that they are gigantic,
while the bed and wardrobe are drastically reduced in
size. And what about those walls?

GOLCONDA

Fat, middle-aged men in bowler hats
are pretty dull. But not when they
pour out of the sky, complete with
umbrellas, like a fantastic army of
saboteurs dropped by the enemy of
our inner security.

PORTRAIT OF MODERN MAN

What is Man? To the minister, priest or rabbi Man is a sinner to be saved. Biologists regard him as an organism. To the anthropologist he is a being to be studied and understood. The doctor sees him as a patient who must be kept healthy. The politician sees him as a voter. In literature, poets and dramatists have made Man the hero of legend—and its villain. Every culture, every century has given its own interpretation of man in its art.

Classically, symbolically, romantically, art has always reflected, through the image of Man, what it thought Man was or might be. Ben Shahn and Andrew Wyeth are among those artists of our time who paint modern man as he is, not compressed into a symbol, not distorted or merely suggested. They give us today's man, as he appears, realistically—harassed, frightened, joyful—in his everyday clothes living his everyday life. They show us man who changes and yet man who remains the same.

ANDREW WYETH

Andrew Wyeth may have inherited his artistic talent from his father N. C. Wyeth, a famous illustrator of children's books. As soon as he could hold a pencil, he began to draw the knights and ladies of the medieval tales his father illustrated. A sickly child, Andrew was tutored at home, and his father, whom he loved and revered, was his only art teacher. Their walks, through the countryside of Chadds Ford, Pennsylvania, became a daily habit that never left him. It was here, and on the coast of Maine, that he studied man and nature—as he does to this day.

His first professional work, done at the age of twelve, was a drawing to decorate an essay written by his father. At sixteen he was attracted by the watercolor paintings of Winslow Homer, famous nineteenth-century American artist, and he set out to master that technique. Three years later he had his first show, in Philadelphia; a year later his show of watercolors in New York was a great success.

Now in his fifties, Wyeth has become probably the most popular and beloved American painter. An exhibition of his paintings in 1960 at the Whitney Museum in New York broke all attendance records and crowds stood in line for hours to see his work. Unchanged by his success, he has kept on working at Chadds Ford and in the Georges River Valley in Maine.

UNSUNG HEROES

The theme, the mood and even the technique of Andrew Wyeth's paintings are set by his subjects. The few square miles near his home in Chadds Ford and his summer place on the coast of Maine gave him all the material he has ever needed. Never traveling abroad, he found his subjects by looking deep into the small worlds around him: the fields, the woods, the sea and the creatures great and small that live in and around them. Most of all, he painted men and women, rugged individuals, whose hard-won victories and painful defeats are visible in their faces, their clothes, even the tools and dishes they use.

There is much solitude, suspense and stillness in Wyeth's paintings. He achieves this effect by bathing his landscapes

CHRISTINA'S WORLD
This woman who drags herself up a barren hillside to
a desolate house has for Wyeth the dignity of a queen.
In his paintings, he championed the courage and
nobility of the men and women who stand up to life,
the people who refuse to surrender in the endless battle
against misfortune and death.

and portraits in a cold, bleak light, the eerie light of a dying sun, just before night falls—perhaps forever. People and animals appear small and insignificant, swallowed up in the forces of nature. The textures of skin and straw, of grindstones and birds' plumage, of weather-beaten houses and faces are caught forever in his work. On his dry, rough, dark surfaces he makes water lighted by a lantern or bright May flowers shine like jewels.

In his intense search to understand the world and men, he becomes the subject he paints, so that he experiences the shape of a tree, of a boat, or a man's face in his bones. "I think," he once said, "that one's art goes as far and as deep as one's love goes."

RACCOON (above)
Wyeth records the significance of the ordinary. The milk pail in an empty shed, the boat abandoned in a meadow, the dogs chained in a barn are clues to mysterious life histories, compressing a place, a time and a life into a sad but loving story.

THE COUNTRY (right)
Each of Wyeth's portraits is a small drama, a frozen moment that tells the life story of someone he admired. His cast of characters includes the unsung heroes that few have had the humanity and talent to recognize and record.

BEN SHAHN

1898—1969

THE RED STAIRWAY (above)
Shahn's war paintings were perhaps the peak of his art.
Here children play in the rubble of a bombed-out street
while a crippled old man climbs a staircase that leads to
nowhere.

CONVERSATIONS (right)
In one of his many lithographs, Shahn comments on the
hypocrisy in our society. One after another, we see the
outer masks fall away to reveal the suspicion and fear.

Ben Shahn was only eight years old when his family left Poland to settle in New York, but his impoverished childhood flavored his work with a sympathy for the downtrodden or alien. He attended high school at night and worked his way through college and art school as a commercial lithographer until 1930.

This background may explain his sympathy for Sacco and Vanzetti, two immigrant shoemakers who were tried for the assassination of a Boston judge. His paintings of the trial won him international fame and revealed his strong feelings about social injustice. In the 1930's he painted murals for the Works Progress Administration (WPA), which employed many artists during the Depression. But most of his paintings were rejected because they were considered too radical. Even when he did posters for the Office of War Information during World War II, he showed his intense feeling for neglected and lonely people.

He was a sensitive writer as well as an artist; he not only wrote several good books on art but also lectured at Harvard University. In 1954 he was chosen as one of two American artists to represent the United States at the international biennial art exhibition in Venice. He died in Roosevelt, New Jersey, in 1969.

PICTURE OF A TROUBLED WORLD

A few artists in every age have tried to paint the social and political events that shaped their age. In the 1930's Ben Shahn chose this theme as his own. "I am interested in life," he said, "and only in art insofar as it enables me to express what I feel about life . . . We live in a time of turmoil too susceptible to drastic and deplorable changes. I feel that the painter who can . . . concern himself with a bowl of pansies or pure abstractions is dodging issues and

is afraid to participate in the life around him." Ben Shahn was never afraid.

The trial and execution of Sacco and Vanzetti, falsely accused, many believe, of a bombing in Boston, decided Ben Shahn's direction. His early experience in making black and white lithographic prints* and his work as a commercial artist helped him paint the shattering portraits of the leading characters in the tragedy. Shahn used the simplicity of so-called folk art* and severe colors to give his painting the effect of a blow.

Turning to the camera, Shahn photographed street scenes around his childhood haunts in Brooklyn and discovered universal meanings in commonplace events. The way he isolates such images in his paintings gives them a powerful effect.

Without sentimentality or sensationalism Ben Shahn succeeded in giving us moving reports on our social and political life. He made us aware of the evil in our world which we must learn to recognize if we are to change it.

LIBERATION (left)
This is a sad comment on the news of peace after World War II. Ragged children whirling on a homemade merry-go-round celebrate the Allied victory in a destroyed Paris street. There is no joy in the scene. Shahn seems to say, "One more such victory will finish us off."

SACCO AND VANZETTI
(overleaf)
A detail from Shahn's mural depicting the trial and execution of Sacco and Vanzetti in 1927 shows how he portrayed every detail of facial expression, body posture, and clothing with an eye to contrasting the poor simple defendants and their aristocratic prosecutors. Every line makes clear his dislike of the Boston judge and other officials who meted out "justice" to the two political dissenters.

PAINTINGS MOVE

We know that all matter is in motion. Each tiny organism has its movements, each microscopic bit of sand has its nucleus circled by atoms. We know that human life begins and ends with the beating of the heart. From earliest childhood we are attracted to a rolling ball, a running puppy, a whirling wheel, a flying plane. Motion has fascinated artists since the cave painters drew running bison and deer. Motion is a sign of life or energy—a force that moves our universe.

Artists in our own time have attempted to suggest motion in painting, such as running lovers, birds in flight, a moving train. In the last century artists, not content to *suggest* motion, have tried to give the direct sensation of movement. The so-called "Futurists," like Umberto Boccioni, did it by inventing forms that gave the feeling of energies imprisoned in figures, landscapes and machines. They used pure spots of color and elongated them to suggest speed and power. "Everything moves" they proclaimed, "all is in a state of flux, of headlong change . . . Objects in movement multiply themselves endlessly and become distorted as they overflow each other like vibrations launched into space and weaving through it." They investigated ways of making color seem to move forward and backward.

Giving art a new direction, Victor Vasarely and Bridget Riley, two leaders in this new way of painting, based their representation of motion on the way our eyes see things, using optical illusions to make paintings move—without motion.

93

UMBERTO BOCCIONI 1882–1916

Umberto Boccioni, a restless, slight man with pleasant, animated features, was born in Reggio, Italy. When his parents insisted that he give up his idea of becoming a painter he left home at sixteen to study with the artist Balla, later a member of the group known as "Futurists."*

In Rome and later in Paris he met the artists with whom he was to be associated for most of his short life. His first show was held in Paris in 1912 and a year later his sculptures were also exhibited there. Because he wanted Italy to enter World War I on the side of the Allies rather than Germany, he was imprisoned for a short time. But in 1916, when Italy joined the Allies, he volunteered for the army. He was killed in a fall from a horse the same year.

THE POWER OF MOVEMENT

Umberto Boccioni was a leader of a group of Italian artists who declared war on traditional art forms. Calling themselves "Futurists," they planned to "glorify the life of today . . . transformed by the victories of science." They were all obsessed with motion. Boccioni did not want to represent arrested movement in his pictures, but the sensation of motion itself. He felt he had to show that all living things are going through constant change and growth. Other movements, too, had to be shown: how light gives the appearance of movement to objects; and even the changes in the mind of the artist painting the picture. He wanted to unite the external appearance of things in motion with their internal spirit—make visible the fact that the flesh and the spirit are one.

Unlike the abstract Cubist painters, Boccioni wanted to maintain his connection with objects as we see them. He aimed at a realism based on what the eye sees as well as on the mental analysis of what it sees. At the same time, he wanted to capture the sense of everything happening at once. In painting the body in motion, Boccioni does not depict the movement of the body by blurring the image or by a series of images such as those made with a slow-motion camera. He created circular forms that roll, undulating forms that move like waves, forms that collide, all of them acting and reacting on each other.

THE CITY RISES
Here Boccioni uses horses, not machines, as the symbol of the power of movement. Employing the colored-dot technique of the French "Pointillists," he turns tame dots into living sparks ejected from a powerful dynamo. The men holding the horses fade out of sight next to the overwhelming power of the horses.

BRIDGET RILEY

1931–

A small, slender, dark woman with the light grace of a dancer, Bridget Riley is probably the most notable woman artist in England. After attending Cheltenham Ladies College and later the Royal College of Art, she did illustrations for a large advertising agency. At the same time she gave instruction to art students and taught in a grammar school in North London.

CURRENT

The entire surface of this painting seems to be in motion. This motion becomes most active in the middle of the canvas, which seems to wave up and down rapidly. If you look at the painting long enough you will see faint colors playing around the most active portions of the canvas. The fact that both motion and color are achieved by simple black vertical lines adds to the force of the painting.

Fascinated by the science of optics and color, which had also inspired the Pointillists,* she began in 1961 to try to create a sense of motion in painting. Her work was represented in various shows in the United States as well as Britain in the 1960's. In 1968, eleven of her paintings—mostly in black and white and composed entirely of straight or curved lines, circles and dots—were shown in the Venice Biennale and won her a first prize.

LINE CREATES COLOR AND MOVEMENT

Michelangelo said that in creating his sculptures he felt he was freeing his figures from the stone. Similarly, Bridget Riley says that when she paints she feels she is freeing the energy imprisoned in forms. Seeking ways to depict energy, Riley does it primarily by creating the appearance of movement in her work. If you put your finger on a Riley painting you will find it still as a stone, but by utilizing the reaction of the eye to form and color, Riley creates not only movement but many different forms of motion. Her paintings undulate, whirl, push out and pull back. They change color, two colors may produce a third, and by varying her tones from black to gray, she manages to produce a sense of depth that moves up and down.

Riley uses the simplest forms, such as dots or small circles, in various sizes, and places them with mathematical regularity on a white surface. After looking at them for a while, you become aware that the black circles are throwing off white circles of light that seem to dance around them like neutrons around a nucleus or planets around the sun. This optical effect is the result of the strain of looking at the regularly spaced black circles and dots and is called the "after-image."

Bridget Riley, by her studies of optics and the reaction of the eye, makes us see the force hidden in color and light and reveals the latent energy in the simplest forms.

CATARACT V

Using a series of blue and red bands on a white background, Riley makes the surface of this painting weave and billow before our eyes. A series of actions and reactions are set in motion, making the stripes seem to advance, recede, bend and twist. She uses variations in tone to accentuate the illusion.

VICTOR VASARELY
1908—

A handsome, slender man with highly refined features, Victor Vasarely was born in Hungary. He went to the School of Medicine in Budapest only to find that he was more interested in painting than in studying anatomy.

In 1929 he joined the branch of the famous Bauhaus school that opened in Hungary, attended the lectures of the Hungarian abstract artist Moholy Nagy, and became acquainted with the work of such artists as Mondrian and the architect Le Corbusier. Since 1930 he has lived in Paris. He became interested in the science of optics as a means of making the spectator aware of his own sensations. Joining a Paris group with similar aims, he began to work on architectural commissions. In the 1950's his work was exhibited in Paris, Brussels, Copenhagen and New York. Today he is in the forefront of artists interested in creating the illusion of motion in painting.

COLOR CREATES MOVEMENT

Believing that discoveries in optics offer new means to create art, Victor Vasarely studied the way the eye is affected by forms, light and color. His aim was to introduce motion into painting, to replace classic perspective by optical illusion and make us experience visually the "invisible" forces of heat, energy, light and color. His paintings are less objects of art than stimulators of sensual responses. His art is therefore more like a continuing event than a finished painting.

In his experiments Vasarely found that line can be transformed into pure vibrations and he finally concluded that form and color are one. All forms are connected with color and every color has qualities of form. Vasarely arrived intuitively at the conclusion that scientists learned through logic—that matter is composed of energy that takes the form of waves and particles constantly alternating.

ORION MC (right) and KALOTA (overleaf)
After you look at Vasarely's paintings for some minutes the colors and patterns suddenly begin to swell, buckle and undulate. Deep cavities and huge bulges appear, and sections of the canvas seem to swirl around a center. Some appear to emit light. In others, colors change their tone as they advance and recede toward contrasting colors. Sometimes an after-image appears on the painting—the same form but in complementary colors. Nothing is stable. Everything is in flux.

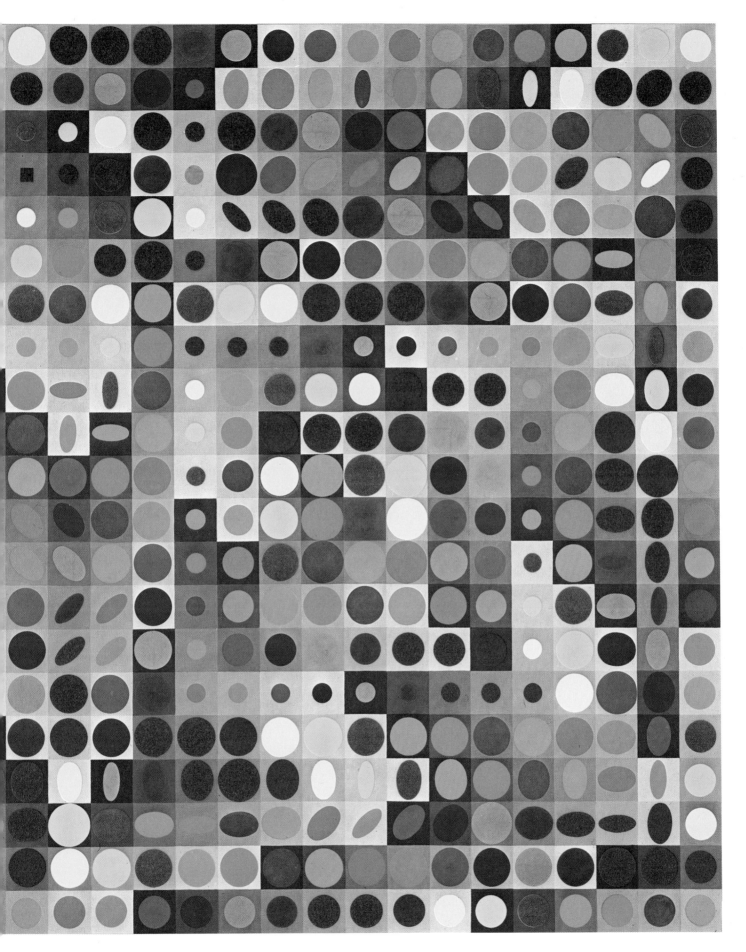

ART
AND
THE
MACHINE

The machine has been the hope and the curse of mankind since it first appeared. Conceived as a means to free man from his bondage to harsh labor, it can easily become a yoke that has done little to improve the lot of millions.

Neither its devotees nor its opponents understood too clearly that the machine was a tool, like other tools, that could be used for good or evil. While many artists, writers and musicians attacked the machine for the new kind of slavery it introduced, and saw it as destroying both man and nature, others clung to the notion that it could free workers and give them the life of gods.

Léger was one of these. It is doubtful that he would admire our polluted cities, our poisoned air, water and earth, or the nuclear bombs invented by our technology. Yet magnificent possibilities still rest with the machine if properly controlled and used. The choice is still ours. In the next few pages, Fernand Léger, the optimist, Roy Lichtenstein, the observer, and Andy Warhol, the pessimist, show us aspects of our machine-dominated civilization.

FERNAND LÉGER

Son of a cattle merchant in Normandy, Fernand Léger set out at nineteen for Paris to earn his living as an architectural draftsman. There he became interested in painting but he failed to pass the entrance examinations at the École des Beaux Arts, so he studied painting with some Paris artists and attended the Academy Julien.

Beginning in 1910 he devoted himself solely to painting. A tawny-haired, stocky man who, someone said, looked "like an English boxer," his sturdiness was apparent in his life and work as well as in his appearance. Serving as a stretcher-bearer in World War I, he was severely gassed and had to be hospitalized for more than a year. After the war he designed costumes and backdrops for the Swedish Ballet and in 1923 for the famous film *Ballet Méchanique*. Leading architects commissioned him to do murals, mosaics, and stained glass walls for various churches and public buildings. In 1952 he designed murals for the United Nations Building in New York. He won first prize at the Sao Paulo Biennale in 1955. Later that year he died in southern France.

MAN AS MACHINE

"The appearance of the modern landscape has been completely transformed visually through the influence of commercial and technical elements," wrote Fernand Léger early in his career. He maintained that "any artistic trend must be a reflection of its time." So machines and the cities built by machines were the themes he explored all his life.

Léger saw the body as only an object with "no more importance than keys or bicycles." He could therefore logically put a portrait of the Mona Lisa together with a close-up of a bunch of keys. He could make a woman look like a robot in a badly fitting suit of armor and present acrobats in the circus as brilliantly colored geometric forms suspended in a space full of cylinders, cones, discs, squares and dots. His clarity of vision and his

LEISURE
Early in his career Léger decided that color was a stunning raw material for painting and as necessary for life as fire and water. The human beings in his paintings appear as though they were bathed in colored lights—an idea that came to him on New York's Broadway, where changing lights from advertising signs flooded the pedestrians in one colored light after another.

inventive imagination carried his art to areas no artist had reached before him.

More optimistic about the machine than most contemporary artists, Léger tried to make its beauty apparent so that our surroundings and work would be more acceptable to us. To the end of his career he still believed that man could be the god of the machine and not its slave.

THE BREAKFAST (above)
Léger's great accomplishment was that he created a new concept of the human figure, recognizable, but having the look of an object with replaceable parts that might have been turned out by a stamping machine.

MECHANICAL ELEMENTS (right)
Léger agreed with Cézanne that everything in nature could be seen in terms of spheres, cones and cylinders. This led him to the abstract art known as Cubism. Fusing his personal Cubism with his idealized machines, he invented "machine beings"—figures with cylinders for torsos, spheres for heads, and pistons for arms and legs. He even saw the movements of men as the rhythms of machine engines.

ANDY WARHOL

1927 —

Andy Warhol is one of the most controversial artists of the 1960's. Immensely enterprising, he is constantly moving into new fields. Slender, pale, with platinum blond hair, Warhol deliberately keeps his background obscure. He was born between 1927 and 1932 in Pennsylvania. His father was a Czechoslovakian coal miner who died while Warhol was still young. As a child Warhol was fond of drawing and later he studied art at the Carnegie Institute of Technology, paying his way by selling fruit and working on window displays for stores.

Moving to New York City when he was twenty-one, he won an award as an advertising illustrator. In 1962 an exhibition of the "New Realists" rocketed him to fame, and his work has since been exhibited around the world. In 1964 he announced that he was a "retired artist" and he began making movies. He has worked in this medium ever since.

MASS-PRODUCED ART

Marcel Duchamp said of Andy Warhol, "If a man takes 59 Campbell soup cans and puts them on canvas, it is not the visual image that concerns us. What interests us is the point of view that wants to put 59 Campbell soup cans on a canvas." Warhol tells us that the effect of mass production and mass media has changed our lives. Our ideas, our tastes, our customs have become chained to machines. Unlike most artists, who paint pictures for a small audience of collectors or museum visitors, Andy Warhol uses mass production methods. Just as advertisers bombard us daily with their art in supermarkets, magazines and newspapers, Warhol uses the machine to get his message to just as large an audience.

Warhol might be called a visual sociologist. In his "factory mades" he gives us a documentary picture of the daily experience of everyman—what he eats, what he loves, what he uses to amuse himself. Nothing in our daily lives escapes him—news events, Hollywood sex symbols, Brillo boxes, cars, death. Like the advertising man, Warhol relies heavily on the appeal of repetition. The pleasure of recognizing a familiar object seems to reassure us that life is stable and reliable. Fifty Campbell soup cans are more reassuring than one. The machine has separated us from nature, made us depend on canned news, canned soup and canned love.

Many Americans are beginning to understand what Warhol is saying. So are collectors—everything he paints is sold.

200 CAMPBELL SOUP CANS

When an art dealer advised Warhol to paint what was most important to
him, he decided to paint soup cans because he had the same soup for lunch
for twenty years. He started painting soup cans and then went on to other
objects of personal importance like Brillo boxes. His studio became a
"factory" where he "mass produced" his paintings.

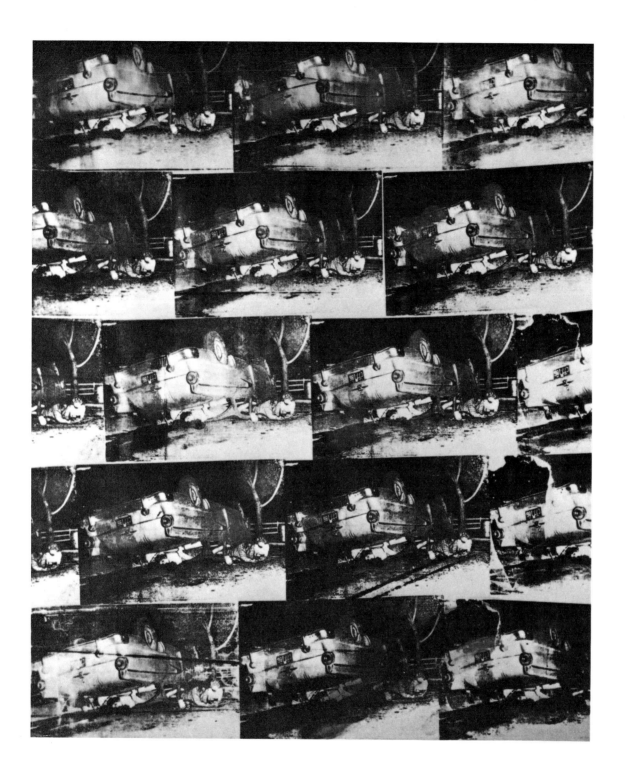

ORANGE DISASTER (above)
Warhol shows us the other side of the automobile
maker's advertisement for the Great American Car—a
crumpled, burning auto with bodies visible in a bloody mess.

MARILYN MONROE (left)
Mass produced, anything can become commonplace.
Even when the subject is the face of Marilyn Monroe,
tens of thousands of reproductions of the Hollywood
sex idol drain it of all allure, beauty and mystery.

ROY LICHTENSTEIN

1923—

Roy Lichtenstein, one of the "New Realists" of the sixties, is a slender man with a pixie face who lives and works in New York's lower East Side. Born in New York City, he studied fine arts at Ohio State University. Later he taught at the New York State College at Oswego and at Rutgers University.

While working on American themes inspired by legends of the Old West, Lichtenstein supported himself by designing window displays and working in sheet metal. He became interested in comic strips when he painted a Mickey Mouse for his young sons in 1960. Before this he had experimented with enlarging the Benday dots that result from the screen technique used to print photographs and color illustrations in newspapers and magazines. Fusing his two interests, this Benday technique finally became his "signature."

In 1962 he was represented in a major exhibition in New York City, and two years later he was among the young artists commissioned to decorate the New York State Pavilion at the 1964 World's Fair. He went on to explore the effects of mixed media,* using metal, plexiglass and other materials painted with acrylics. He even designed the advertising billboards for "Expo '67" in Montreal. The wide appeal of his style was evident in the way his work was enthusiastically received by both critics and the public when it was shown at the Tate Gallery in London in 1968.

PAINTING WITH PRINTING PROCESS DOTS

While the machine has been turning out streams of commercial art on billboards and in magazines and newspaper advertising for years, no one used these machine reproductions as a subject for art until Roy Lichtenstein came along. He wanted not only to get away from the hand-painted brush stroke of conventional painting but to make his art look as if it had actually been done by a machine.

He was fascinated by Benday dots. The Pointillists had painted their pictures with tiny dots of pure color. The Benday dot did the same thing, only by machine. Why not use the Benday dot to paint

pictures? Although Lichtenstein imitated this dot by hand, using a screen* for the dots, his art had the look of a machine product.

He went on to paint pictures in the manner of Cézanne and Picasso, using his dot technique to give them a machine quality. Sunsets, landscapes, seascapes came off his easel in the same technique. Many of these were indeed totally machine-made, being manufactured in enamel or metal. Most recently he has been using billboards for paintings whose scale, color and impersonal handling are also like outdoor posters. By making the raw material of commercial art the subject of his paintings, Lichtenstein gives us a fresh view of our machine age—and its potentials for painting.

PISTOL (left) and
DAWNING (above)
Simplified forms and "sock-it-to-them" instant readability are the basis of advertising art and illustration. Lichtenstein increases these effects by eliminating all details, emphasizing his forms with heavy outlines, using solid-colored shadows, metallic highlights, and the brash, vivid tones of advertising art.

LIVE AMMO (BLANG) (below)
and GIRL (right)
At first, Lichtenstein used comic strips
for his images because to him "they
summed up the essence of our times."
Dealing with war, murder, love, hate,
the comic strip presented themes that
attracted the greatest mass audience.
They had little relationship to real life
but their exaggerations made them
easy to follow, especially for people
whose own lives are humdrum and
colorless.

GLOSSARY

ABSTRACT EXPRESSIONISM

A broad range of painting styles that appeared around 1945 in New York City. The Abstract Expressionists used a spontaneous, emotional (expressionistic) approach in creating a picture, and the paintings usually do not represent figures, forms or objects as they appear in nature. Jackson Pollock (p. 22), Willem de Kooning (p. 60) and Hans Hofmann (p. 48) are Abstract Expressionist painters.

ARABESQUE

A type of decoration using flowing patterns of flowers, leaves, branches, scroll-work, etc. fancifully intertwined.

CLASSIC ART

Art which has those qualities of Greek or Roman style, such as reason, discipline, restraint, order. It is sometimes explained as a mixture of simplicity, harmony and proportion.

COLLAGE

A picture or design made by pasting materials like colored paper, newsprint, photographs, string, rags, rope, wire or hair on canvas or board, sometimes with a figure drawn or painted over the assembled material.

CUBISM

A movement led by Picasso (p. 14) and George Braque, which tried to liberate form. Influenced by Cézanne (p. 8), the Cubists saw the basic structure behind reality as made up of basic geometric shapes such as the cube, the cylinder and the cone. By arranging these geometric elements, the Cubists created new combinations of basic forms; see Picasso's *The Young Women of Avignon* (p. 14) and *The Three Musicians* (p. 16).

ETCHING

A graphic process in which a copper plate is covered with a layer of wax and lines are cut through this layer by a needle. The plate is then dipped into acid, which attacks only those portions of the plate which have been exposed by the needle, leaving the wax-protected portion of the plate unaffected.

EXPRESSIONISM

Art in which the personal emotions of the artist are of major importance, as in the paintings of Van Gogh (p. 30). The modern Expressionist movement began with Edvard Munch (p. 52), whose work had great influence in Germany where the Expressionist groups "The Bridge" and "The Blue Rider" were founded. Other Expressionist painters associated with these groups were Soutine (p. 56), Kirchner (p. 58) and Klee (p. 74).

FAUVES

French word meaning "wild beasts," used to describe a group of French artists, led by Matisse (p. 42), who used violent, uncontrolled, brilliant color.

FEDERAL ART PROJECT

Established in 1935 as part of the U.S. Works Projects Administration during the Depression, this was a government program which employed artists who were in financial need. It employed over five thousand persons and produced more than 140,000 works of art.

FOLK ART

The native pictures, pottery, sculpture, etc., produced by professionally untrained people in all parts of the world.

FORM

The structure in a work of art whereby the artist's conception and vision are brought to life. This varies from the purely representational, or realistic, to the purely abstract.

FUTURISTS

A group of Italian artists who published a manifesto in 1910 declaring war on traditional art forms. They planned to "glorify the life of today . . . transformed by the victories of science." They were obsessed with motion, and tried to paint dynamic action.

IMPRESSIONISM

A movement or style of painting which began in the 1860s, and is generally considered to mark the beginning of the modern art movement. The Impressionists tried to capture a fleeting *impression* of nature, as if seen for the first time. They showed that color changes with the light that is cast on it, and that changing light also changes the form of objects. This was a break with the painting of the past, which had regarded natural colors and forms as unchanging.

JAPANESE PRINTS

Japanese color prints first appeared in France in the 1860s, and were admired by artists for their fresh view of nature. The subject matter—usually actors or landscapes—portrayed the real world and often expressed deep emotion. The use of flat areas of color and the technique of viewing from unusual angles seemed like daring innovations. Japanese influences can be seen in Van Gogh (p. 30) and Cézanne (p. 8).

LANDSCAPE PAINTING

Painting that represents natural scenery, such as fields, hills, forests, water.

LITHOGRAPHIC PRINT

A print made from a lithographic stone or a prepared zinc plate on which a drawing has been made with greasy crayons or ink. It is then pressed onto the paper which picks up the ink.

MEDIUM

The particular material with which an art work is made: oils, watercolor, chalks, pen and ink, etc.

MIXED MEDIA

The mixing of materials, such as metals or plastics, with oils, watercolor or pen and ink in a work of art.

MURAL

A decorative picture which is painted on a wall or fastened to a wall surface.

OP(tical) ART

A term that came into use in the 1960s to describe the work of such painters as Victor Vasarely (p. 98) and Bridgit Riley (p. 96). Op Art relies on purely visual reactions, especially optical illusions. Op Art paintings are generally a mass of shapes, lines or vivid colors that seem to shift constantly under the eye.

PERSPECTIVE

A scientific method (dating from the Renaissance) used by artists to create the illusion of depth. It makes natural objects and figures in the distance look the way we actually see them in real life.

PIGMENT

The coloring substances, usually in powder form, which are mixed or ground with liquids (such as water or oil) to make paint.

POINTILLISM

From the French word, *pointiller*, meaning to dot or stipple. Pointillism consists of putting separate spots, or dots, of pure color, side by side on a canvas. When seen at the right distance, the spectator's eye will automatically mix the colors, so that red and yellow produce the sensation of orange, and red and blue produce the sensation of mauve.

POP ART

Starting in England in the 1950s, Pop Art emerged in the United States during the 1960s as a reaction against Abstract Expressionism. Influenced by Marcel Duchamp (p. 20), pop artists were concerned with their everyday environment, and took their images—coke bottles, movie stars, soup cans, comic strips—from popular culture. Andy Warhol (p. 106) and Roy Lichtenstein (p. 110) are major pop artists.

POST-IMPRESSIONISM

A period in modern painting that started in the middle 1880s, coming between Impressionism and the beginnings of Fauvism, Cubism and Expressionism in the early twentieth century. Post-Impressionism was a reaction against Impressionism, which emphasized the purely visual, external effect of light or movement. Cézanne (p. 8), Gauguin (p. 36), Van Gogh (p. 30) and Matisse (42) are called post-impressionists.

RENAISSANCE

A period in the history of art, mainly the fourteenth and fifteenth centuries. At first a revival (literally "rebirth") of Greek and Roman models in literature, architecture and sculpture, it became an intense desire for knowledge and an awareness of the dignity and humanity of the individual. It began in Italy and reached its height in the visual arts with Michelangelo, Raphael and Leonardo da Vinci.

REPRESENTATIONAL ART

Painting or sculpture which tries to reproduce the physical appearance of objects or persons as we actually see them.

SALON

Annual exhibitions of painting and sculpture in France.

SALON DES INDEPENDENTS

An unofficial "independent" salon organized by a group of painters in France who were refused admittance by the official salon group in 1884.

SILK SCREEN

A method of color reproduction, often used commercially for the reproduction of posters and billboards. The design or picture to be reproduced is broken up into its chief colors. A frame is then prepared for each color, representing the shape of the area which the color will cover. Paint is then squeezed through the screens onto the printing paper.

STILL LIFE PAINTING

A painting made up of inanimate objects such as pottery, fruit, flowers.

STYLE

An artist's manner of expressing himself in his painting. This term is also used in a more general sense to describe the characteristic manner of a period of art, such as Renaissance style or Impressionist style.

SURREALISM

From the French word meaning "super-reality"—the reality of the dreams, fantasies and imaginings that make up the major part of our subconscious minds. The movement was officially begun in 1924, when the first Surrealist Manifesto declared that it was the artist's duty to free man's unconscious personality from reason and inhibition. The movement was deeply influenced by the theories of Sigmund Freud.

WATERCOLOR

A form of transparent water painting in which the white of the paper provides the light areas, and no white paint is used.

WOODCUT

A method of taking a print from the surface of a wood block. A design is drawn on the block, and the parts the artist does not wish to be printed are carved away. Ink is rolled on the surface and it is pressed onto paper which picks up the design of the raised surface.

Index of Artists, Pictures and Owners

Artists are listed alphabetically; works are listed in the order in which they appear in the section devoted to each artist. Color plates are starred.

The author and publishers wish to thank all individuals and institutions who have made works of art in their possession available for reproduction. Unless otherwise indicated in parenthesis, photographs were supplied by the owners.

This book was planned and prepared
by Chanticleer Press

Publisher: Paul Steiner
Editor: Milton Rugoff
Associate: Connie Sullivan
Art Director: Ulrich Ruchti,
assisted by Elaine Jones
Production: Gudrun Buettner,
assisted by Ruth Charnes